To Nina and Sam, for their sense of fun,
and with acknowledgments to a lot of
anonymous people and an onymous one,
Chris Leeds, author of 'English Humour'
(Belin, Paris, 1989).

By the same author

WeEuropeans

EuroManagers & Martians

The NewComers

Great Britain Little England

For details, see back of book

Published by Europublications, Division of Europublic SA/NV,
Avenue Winston Churchill 11, (box 21), B-1180 Brussels.
Tel: + 32 2 343 77 26, Fax: + 32 2 343 93 30.

Copyright © Richard Hill   Cover: Kath Walker

Translations: Albacourt

Printed in Belgium. Edition et Imprimerie, Brussels.

D/1995/6421/3

A Division of Europublic SA/NV

Have you heard this one?

An Anthology of European Jokes

in English * in het Nederlands
* en Français * in Deutsch

collected and commented by Richard Hill

Here are some of the better jokes we Europeans tell about one another. There are a lot of bad ones - far too many - but, if I have done my work properly, you will find none of them here (that depends of course on your 'cultural programming' and perception, which is what these jokes are all about).

These are all jokes that have been recounted by others, mainly *viva voce* to me in person, occasionally in writing. While I claim copyright for this book and my comments, I have no claim on the jokes themselves: they revert to the public domain whence they come.

Good European jokes are neither stupid nor abusive. They tell you something instructive about the way people from different cultures perceive one another. And some of these jokes shed light on the cultures of both the 'sender' and the 'receiver'.

As that eminent European Johann Wolfgang von Goethe said, rather severely: "There is nothing in which people more betray their character than in what they laugh at". Taken in the right spirit, humour is an excellent starting point for cross-cultural comprehension.

※ ☞

Voor u liggen een aantal van de betere grappen die wij Europeanen over elkaar vertellen. Slechte grappen zijn legio, maar als wij in onze opzet geslaagd zijn, zult u die hier niet vinden, maar dat is natuurlijk weer afhankelijk van uw 'eigen culturele plaatje' en benadering en dat is nu precies waar het bij deze grappen om draait.

Het zijn allemaal grappen die mij door anderen verteld zijn of soms voor mij werden opgeschreven. Ik behoud me weliswaar de rechten voor op dit boek en het door mij geleverde commentaar, maar de grappen zelf zijn niet mijn eigendom en behoren tot het gedachtengoed waaraan ze ontsproten zijn.

Goede Europese grappen hebben als kenmerk dat ze niet dom zijn en ook niet beledigend. Ze brengen u iets bij over hoe mensen met een verschillende culturele achtergrond over elkaar denken. En er zijn grappen die een verhelderend licht werpen op de culturen van zowel de 'zender' als de 'ontvanger'.

Of zoals een van de grote Europeanen bij uitstek, Johann Wolfgang von Goethe, het nogal streng zei: "niets verraadt meer over het karakter van de mensen dan wat ze aan het lachen maakt". Humor zonder bijbedoelingen is een uitstekende voedingsbodem voor onderling cultureel begrip.

4

Voici une sélection des bonnes blagues que nous autres Européens nous racontons les uns sur les autres. Il en existe beaucoup de mauvaises - beaucoup trop - mais, si j'ai bien travaillé, vous n'en trouverez ici aucune (bien entendu, cela dépend de votre façon de percevoir les choses et de votre "programmation culturelle", ce qui constitue justement le sujet des blagues).

Toutes ces blagues sont le fait d'autrui. La plupart du temps, elles m'ont été racontées de vive voix, parfois par écrit. Si je revendique un droit d'auteur pour ce livre et mes commentaires, je n'ai aucune prétention quant aux blagues elles-mêmes : venues du domaine public, elles y retournent.

Les bonnes blagues européennes ne sont ni stupides, ni injurieuses. Elles vous instruisent sur la manière dont les personnes de cultures différentes se perçoivent les unes les autres. Certaines de ces histoires éclairent d'ailleurs aussi bien la culture de l'"expéditeur" que celle du "destinataire".

Comme l'éminent Européen Johann Wolfgang von Goethe le disait assez sévèrement : "Il n'y a rien dans lequel les personnes révèlent davantage leur caractère que dans ce avec quoi ils rient." Pris dans le bon sens, l'humour constitue un excellent point de départ de la compréhension transculturelle.

❧ ❦

Hier sind einige der besseren Witze, die wir Europäer über andere Europäer erzählen. Es gibt viele - viel zu viele - schlechte Witze, aber wenn wir gut gewählt haben, dann werden Sie diesen hier nicht begegnen (was natürlich auch wieder von Ihrer eigenen "kulturellen Programmierung" und Wahrnehmung abhängt, denn gerade darum geht es ja bei diesen Scherzen).

Es sind insgesamt Witze, die von anderen weitererzählt worden sind, hauptsächlich mir und meistens viva voce, manchmal auch schriftlich. Für dieses Buch und meine Kommentare nehme ich zwar Urheberrechte in Anspruch, aber nicht für die Witze an sich, denn diese gehen an die Allgemeinheit zurück, dorthin wo sie hergekommen sind.

Gute europäische Witze sind weder dumm noch beleidigend. Sie sind aufschlußreich und zeigen uns, wie die verschiedenen Kulturen einander wahrnehmen. Dabei werfen einige dieser Witze etwas Licht auf beide betroffenen Kulturen, und zwar sowohl die des "Absenders" als auch die des "Empfängers".

Wie der große Europäer Johann Wolfgang von Goethe bereits, etwas streng, behauptete: "Mit nichts verraten die Menschen ihren Charakter mehr als mit dem über das sie lachen". Mit der richtigen Einstellung dient der Humor als hervorragender Ausgangspunkt für ein kulturenüberschreitendes Verständnis.

This is the **original** European joke, still funny but somewhat out-of-date, particularly in the 'hell' scenario: the German police (depending on whom you talk to) can be wonderful, British chefs are sometimes brilliant, French mechanics are magicians and the Italians, when they want to, can organise things better than anyone else. The only ones left to challenge their stereotype are the Swiss (but they have their own version of the joke where, in the 'hell' scenario, the Germans are the comedians).

Heaven is where the police are British,
the chefs French, the mechanics German,
the lovers Italian
and it is all organised by the Swiss.

Hell is where the police are German,
the chefs British, the mechanics French,
the lovers Swiss
and it is all organised by the Italians.

❧ ❧

Dit moet wel een van de eerste Europese grappen geweest zijn. Nog steeds geestig, dat wel, maar ten aanzien van hoe men zich de hel moet voorstellen, misschien toch wat achterhaald. Immers de Duitse politie kan (uitzonderingen daargelaten) uitermate voorkomend zijn, er bestaan tegenwoordig Britse koks die kunnen toveren, er zijn Franse monteurs met gouden handen en als Italianen zich er werkelijk toe zetten, is hun organisatie vlekkeloos. Ons is slechts een helse zekerheid gebleven: liefde op z'n Zwitsers (maar de Zwitsers hebben hun eigen variant van deze grap en in deze versie wordt de humor in de hel verzorgd door de Duitsers).

In de hemel is de politie Brits, zijn de koks Frans, de ingenieurs Duits, is de liefde een Italiaanse zaak en is de organisatie in handen van de Zwitsers.

In de hel is de politie Duits, doen de Britten het eten, staan de Fransen in voor de techniek, bepalen de Zwitsers wat liefde is en dat alles wordt dan geregeld door de Italianen.

Voici la vraie blague européenne, toujours amusante mais quelque peu dépassée, surtout au niveau du "scénario de l'enfer". La police allemande peut être sympathique (cela dépend sur qui vous tombez), les chefs britanniques sont parfois brillants, les mécaniciens français sont des magiciens et les Italiens - quand ils le veulent - savent organiser les choses mieux que quiconque. Les seuls qui doivent encore faire mentir le stéréotype sont les Suisses... (mais ils ont leur propre version de la blague, où, dans le "scénario de l'enfer", les Allemands sont les comédiens).

Le **paradis**, c'est là ou les policiers sont britanniques,
les chefs français, les mécaniciens allemands,
les amoureux italiens,
et où l'ensemble est organisé par les Suisses.

L'**enfer**, c'est là ou les policiers sont allemands,
les chefs britanniques, les mécaniciens français,
les amoureux suisses,
et où l'ensemble est organisé par les Italiens.

Hier geht es um den ursprünglichen europäischen Witz, der zwar speziell im Zusammenhang mit dem Begriff der "Hölle" etwas altmodisch wirkt, aber dennoch sehr lustig geblieben ist. Dazu folgendes : die deutsche Polizei kann wunderbar sein (was von Ihrem Gesprächspartner abhängen dürfte), britische Chefköche sind manchmal großartig, französische Mechaniker können Wunder vollbringen und die Italiener sind, wenn sie wollen, die allergrößten Organisationstalente. Die einzigen, die ihr stereotypisches Image noch anfechten, sind die Schweizer ... (aber diese erzählen den Witz in ihrer eigenen Fassung, in der die Deutschen in der "Hölle" die Komiker sind).

Im **Himmel** arbeiten die Briten als Polizisten, die Franzosen als Küchenchefs, die Deutschen als Mechaniker, die Italiener als Liebhaber und das alles wird von den Schweizern organisiert !

In der **Hölle** arbeiten die Deutschen als Polizisten, die Briten als Küchenchefs, die Franzosen als Mechaniker, die Schweizer als Liebhaber und das alles wird von den Italienern organisiert !

Unfortunately, it's downhill from here on. Other pan-European jokes are much more laboured and mildly abusive, referring to things like French humility, German charm, Italian courage, Dutch generosity, Belgian road manners, Swiss gaiety, Scandinavian wit and Greek sensitivity. Here's one which says much the same things, but more tactfully.

The captain of a sinking ship had difficulty in persuading his European passengers to jump in the water. So, as he explained afterwards, he appealed to the dominant instincts in each of the nationalities: "I told the English it would be unsporting not to jump, the French that it would be the smart thing to do, the Germans that it was an order... and the Italians that jumping overboard was prohibited".

❦ ❦

Jammergenoeg is het gehalte van de grappen er sindsdien niet op vooruit gegaan. De meeste grappen over Europeanen zijn veel krampachtiger en een tikkeltje beledigend. Ze verwijzen naar de nederigheid van de Fransen, de charme van de Duitsers, de moed van de Italianen, de vrijgevigheid van de Hollanders, Belgische heren in het verkeer, het spontaan plezier van de Zwitsers, de geestigheid van de Scandinaviërs en de fijngevoeligheid van de Grieken.

Deze grap gaat over hetzelfde, maar dan zonder botte bijl...

Op een zinkend schip had de kapitein de grootste moeite om zijn Europese passagiers zover te krijgen dat ze overboord sprongen. Later vertelde hij hoe hij uiteindelijk dan maar een beroep gedaan had op de diepere instincten die elk van de nationaliteiten eigen zijn: 'Tegen de Engelsen zei ik dat niet springen uitermate onsportief zou zijn, de Fransen verzekerde ik dat ze daarmee zouden bewijzen hoe pienter ze wel waren, de Duitsers beval ik te springen...en de Italianen verbood ik te springen'.

Malheureusement, les choses se dégradent à partir d'ici. D'autres blagues paneuropéennes sont beaucoup plus laborieuses et quelque peu injurieuses, car elles évoquent des sujets tels que l'humilité française, le charme allemand, le courage italien, la générosité néerlandaise, la courtoisie des Belges au volant, la gaîté suisse, la finesse scandinave et la sensibilité grecque. En voici une qui dit à peu près la même chose, mais avec un peu plus de tact.

Le capitaine d'un bateau en perdition avait des difficultés à convaincre ses passagers européens de se jeter à l'eau. C'est pourquoi, comme il l'expliqua par la suite, il fit appel aux instincts dominants de chaque nationalité : "J'ai dit aux Anglais que ce ne serait pas sportif de ne pas sauter, aux Français que ce serait la chose la plus intelligente à faire, aux Allemands que c'était un ordre... et aux Italiens qu'il était interdit de sauter par-dessus bord."

※ ❧

Leider geht es von hier aus bergab, denn andere paneuropäische Witze wirken manchmal etwas "an den Haaren herbeigezogen" und leicht beleidigend; wenn Eigenschaften erwähnt werden wie, beispielsweise, die französische Bescheidenheit, der deutsche Charme, der italienische Mut, die holländische Freigebigkeit, das belgische Verhalten im Straßenverkehr, die Lustigkeit der Schweizer, die skandinavische Schlagfertigkeit und die griechische Einfühlsamkeit. Es folgt ein Witz, der etwa das gleiche, nur etwas taktvoller, zum Ausdruck bringt.

Der Kapitän eines sinkenden Schiffs kann seine europäischen Passagiere nur schwer dazu bewegen, ins Wasser zu springen. Wie er später erzählt, appellierte er in dieser Lage an die vorherrschenden Triebe jeder einzelnen Nationalität : "Dem Engländer erklärte ich, es sei unsportlich, nicht zu springen, dem Franzosen, es wäre schlau, wenn er spränge, den Deutschen, es wäre ein Befehl ... und den Italienern schließlich, es wäre verboten, über Bord zu springen ...".

Ships come into a lot of European jokes, including this British one. British humour tends to be self-deprecatory, a natural extension of the Englishman's flair for inverted snobbery and, by implication, snobbery itself. While it is permissible to tell jokes against the British in their presence, choose carefully.

During a NATO naval exercise, three senior officers - German, French and British - are on the deck of the flagship arguing about bravery.

"I will show you what is bravery", says the German, calling one of his men: "Schmidt, climb the ship's mast and jump into the water". The German sailor climbs the mast, jumps into the water - and sinks like a stone.

"This we can do better", says the Frenchman and summons one of his men: "Dupont, climb the mast and jump". Dupont obliges and jumps, landing in a bloody heap on the deck.

"Um er", says the British officer, "Jones, would you mind showing these gentlemen how brave the British are?". "Not bloody likely", responds Able Seaman Jones. "There, gentlemen", says the officer, "how's that for bravery?".

❧ ❧

Heel wat Europese grappen gaan over schepen, ook deze. Britse humor neemt zichzelf op de hak en dat houdt dan weer verband met de aanleg van de Engelsen voor omgekeerd snobisme, wat ook een vorm van snobisme is. Een tegen de Britten gerichte grap vertellen waar ze bij zijn, màg, maar het blijft uitkijken:

Tijdens een marine-oefening van de NAVO ontspint zich op het dek van het vlaggeschip tussen drie hoge officieren, een Duitser, een Fransman en een Brit, een discussie over dapperheid. "Ik zal u tonen wat dapperheid is, zegt de Duitser en roept één van zijn manschappen: "Schmidt, klim in de mast en spring in het water". De Duitse matroos klimt in de mast, springt in het water... en zinkt als een baksteen. "Dat doen wij beter", zegt de Fransman en laat één van zijn mannen komen: "Dupont, klim in de mast en spring". Dupont gehoorzaamt en springt...en eindigt als een bloederig hoopje ellende op het dek.

"Ahum", zegt de Britse officier, "Jones, zou jij zo vriendelijk willen zijn de heren te laten zien hoe dapper wij Britten zijn ?" "Van z'n leven niet", luidde het antwoord van zeevarend matroos Jones. "Kijk, heren", zegt de officier, "als dat niet dapper is ?"

Les bateaux interviennent dans un grand nombre de blagues européennes, y compris dans cette blague britannique. L'humour britannique tend à l'auto-dérision, prolongement naturel du don inné des Anglais pour le snobisme à l'envers et, par conséquent, pour le snobisme lui-même. S'il est permis de raconter des blagues sur les Britanniques en leur présence, choisissez-les tout de même prudemment.

Au cours d'un exercice naval de l'OTAN, trois officiers supérieurs - un Allemand, un Français et un Britannique - se trouvent sur le pont du bâtiment amiral, où ils débattent au sujet de la bravoure. "Je vais vous montrer ce qu'est la bravoure", dit l'Allemand, en appelant un de ses hommes : "Schmidt, grimpez au mât du navire et sautez dans l'eau". Le marin allemand grimpe au mât, saute dans l'eau - et coule à pic. "Nous pouvons faire mieux", dit le Français, et il ordonne à un de ses hommes : "Dupont, grimpez au mât et sautez". Dupont obtempère et saute. Il s'écrase sur le pont dans une mare de sang. "Hem", dit l'officier britannique, "Jones, auriez-vous l'obligeance de montrer à ces gentlemen comme les Britanniques sont braves ?". "Cause toujours", répond le matelot. "Eh bien, messieurs", dit l'officier, "ne voilà-t-il pas une belle preuve de bravoure ?"

❧ ❧

Schiffe kommen in vielen europäischen Witzen vor, auch in diesem Beispiel britischen Humors, der dazu neigt, die eigene Person herabzuwürdigen, was wiederum im Zusammenhang mit dem Flair der Engländer für eine gewisse Art von Snobismus und, implizite, für gerade diesen Snobismus zu betrachten ist.

Bei einer Marineübung der NATO stehen drei hohe Offiziere - ein Deutscher, ein Franzose und eine Engländer - auf dem Deck des Flaggschiffes und unterhalten sich angeregt über Mut und Tapferkeit. "Ich werde Ihnen zeigen, was Tapferkeit ist", sagt der Deutsche und befiehlt einem seiner Leute: "Schmidt, steigen Sie auf den Mast und springen Sie ins Wasser !" Der deutsche Seemann steigt auf den Mast, springt ins Wasser und sackt weg wie ein Stein. "Das können wir besser", sagt der Franzose und zitiert einen seiner Männer herbei: "Dupont, steigen Sie auf den Mast und springen Sie herunter." Dupont führt den Befehl aus und springt auf das Deck, ein blutendes Häufchen Elend. "Nun denn", sagt der englische Offizier, "Jones, würde es Ihnen etwas ausmachen, diesen Herren zu zeigen, wie tapfer die Engländer sind?". "Fällt mir nicht ein", gibt der Vollmatrose Jones zur Antwort. "Na also, meine Herren", sagt der Offizier, "hat der Mann Mut oder nicht ?"

It is strange how much European folklore revolves around holes in the ground. The Pied Piper of Hamlin (Hameln) took the children underground and brought them up in the Siebenburgen region of Romania. Jules Verne had his explorers go underground in Iceland (in *'Journey to the Centre of the Earth'*) and come up in Sicily. And a lot of European ethnic jokes find their scenarios in caves...

A Swede, a Norwegian and a Dane are caught in a snowstorm on the side of a mountain. They stumble across a cave and decide to take shelter. On entering they are greeted by an awful stench which, on inspection, turns out to come from a half-dead goat which has taken refuge in the cave. The three of them debate what to do and the Norwegian agrees to go in first. Five minutes later he staggers out sick with nausea and collapses. Then the Dane goes in and, ten minutes later, crawls out and expires. Finally the Swede goes in and, fifteen minutes later... the goat comes out.

❦ ❧

Het is opvallend hoeveel van de Europese folklore zich afspeelt rond een gat in de grond. De rattenvanger van Hamelen nam de kinderen mee onder de grond en ze kwamen weer boven in Siebenburgen ergens in Roemenië. Jules Verne laat zijn ontdekkingsreizigers in IJsland onder de grond gaan (in *"De reis naar het midden van de aarde"*) en ze komen in Sicilië weer boven de grond. En heel wat Europese grappen met een etnische ondertoon spelen zich af in holen en grotten...

Een Zweed, een Noor en een Deen komen in een sneeuwstorm terecht. Ze ontdekken een grot en besluiten daar te wachten tot het voorbij is. In de grot heerst een afgrijselijke stank, die afkomstig blijkt te zijn van een halfdode geit die zich daar verstopt heeft. Met z'n drieën bespreken ze wat hen te doen staat en de Noor stemt toe als eerste naar binnen te gaan. Vijf minuten later komt hij kotsmisselijk weer naar buiten en stort in elkaar. Dus gaat de Deen naar binnen en hij kruipt tien minuten later naar buiten en legt het loodje. Als laatste gaat de Zweed naar binnen en een kwartier later... komt de geit naar buiten.

Il est étrange de constater combien le folklore européen fait allusion aux trous dans le sol. Le Joueur de flûte de Hameln a entraîné les enfants sous terre et les a ramenés à la surface dans la région de Siegenburgen, en Roumanie. Jules Verne fait descendre ses explorateurs sous terre en Islande (dans *"Voyage au centre de la terre"*) et les fait ressortir en Sicile. Et de nombreuses blagues sur les peuples d'Europe se déroulent dans des grottes...

Un Suédois, un Norvégien et un Danois sont surpris par une tempête de neige sur le flanc d'une montagne. Ils découvrent une grotte et décident de s'y abriter. Lorsqu'ils y pénètrent, ils sont surpris par une atroce puanteur qui, après inspection, se révèle provenir d'un bouc à moitié mort qui s'est réfugié dans la grotte. Les trois hommes se concertent et le Norvégien décide d'entrer le premier. Cinq minutes plus tard, il sort en titubant et s'évanouit. Le Danois essaie à son tour. Dix minutes plus tard, il ressort à quatre pattes et s'écroule. Enfin, le Suédois entre dans la grotte... un quart-d'heure plus tard, le bouc se précipite dehors.

❧ ❦

Es ist merkwürdig, wieviel europäische Folklore um Löcher in der Erde zu kreisen scheint. Der Rattenfänger von Hameln führte die Kinder unter die Erde und brachte sie in der Gegend von Siebenbürgen in Rumänien wieder ans Tageslicht. Jules Verne ließ seine Forschungsreisenden in Island in die unterirdische Welt verschwinden (in der *"Reise zum Mittelpunkt der Erde"*) und zum Vorschein kamen sie dann wieder in Sizilien. Eine ganze Menge europäischer ethnischer Witze spielen sich in Höhlen ab ...

Ein Schwede, ein Norweger und ein Däne werden am Berg von einem Schneesturm überrascht. Sie stolpern in eine Höhle und beschließen, dort Schutz zu suchen. Am Höhleneingang bereits schlägt ihnen ein fürchterlicher Gestank entgegen. Sie gehen diesem Gestank nach und stoßen auf einen halbtoten Ziegenbock, der Zuflucht in der Höhle gesucht hat. Alle drei diskutieren dann darüber, was zu machen sei, und der Norweger erklärt sich bereit, als erster hineinzugehen. Fünf Minuten später wankt er aus der Höhle, es wird ihm übel und er fällt ohnmächtig zusammen. Dann geht der Däne hinein, kriecht zehn Minuten später heraus und bricht zusammen. Schließlich begibt der Schwede sich in die Höhle und fünfzehn Minuten später ... rennt der Ziegenbock heraus.

It may have something to do with our innate sense of insecurity. We have Angst, we search endlessly for an identity, or we just worry. More often than not, we worry about money.

Some Europeans are better at this than others: for example the Scots, the Dutch (who have too flat a country for mountain caves), the Galicians of northwestern Spain, the Galitzianers of Poland and, of all people, the Pontic Greeks (the ones who, if you're coming from the South Pole, are on your right when you get to the Black Sea).

So-and-so (Scot, Pontic Greek, etc) survives a plane crash on a desolate mountain. He or she, hungry and exhausted, finds shelter in a cave. A Red Cross search party climbs up the mountain, spots the cave entrance and calls: 'Anyone in there?' "Who's that?", comes the reply. "Red Cross", says the leader of the search party, "Thank you", comes the reply, "I've already donated".

❦ ❦

Misschien heeft het iets te maken met ons aangeboren gevoel van onzekerheid. We worden door angst beheerst. We zijn onophoudelijk op zoek naar onze identiteit of we maken ons zorgen. En waar we ons het meeste zorgen over maken is geld.

Sommige Europeanen zijn hier bijzonder sterk in. De Schotten, bij voorbeeld, de Nederlanders (het land is te plat voor grotten in de bergen), de Galiciërs in het noord-westen van Spanje, de Poolse Galiciërs en, dat kon niet missen, de Pontische Grieken (wanneer u aan de Zwarte Zee bent, komend van de Zuidpool, zijn het de Grieken aan uw rechterhand).

Dinges (Schot, Pontische Griek, enz.) blijkt de enige overlevende te zijn als zijn vliegtuig neerstort tegen een afgelegen berg. Hij heeft honger en is de uitputting nabij, maar vindt een grot om te schuilen. Een reddingsploeg van het Rode Kruis beklimt de berg, komt bij de ingang van de grot en roept: "Is daar iemand?" "Wie is daar?" wordt er gevraagd. "Het Rode Kruis", zegt de leider van de reddingsploeg. "Nee, dank u, ik heb al gegeven", komt het antwoord.

Peut-être est-ce dû à notre sentiment inné d'insécurité. Nous éprouvons de l'"Angst", nous cherchons sans cesse une identité, ou nous nous faisons simplement du souci. Et très souvent, nous nous tracassons pour de l'argent.

Certains Européens se soucient plus d'argent que d'autres, p. ex. les Ecossais, les Néerlandais (dont le pays est trop plat pour avoir des grottes), les Galiciens du nord-ouest de l'Espagne, les Galiciens de Pologne, et surtout les Grecs pontiques (ceux qui sont à votre droite lorsque, venant du pôle sud, vous arrivez à la Mer Noire).

M. Untel (Ecossais, Grec pontique, etc.) survit à un crash aérien sur une montagne déserte. Affamé et exténué, il trouve refuge dans une grotte. Une équipe de secours de la Croix-Rouge escalade la montagne, découvre l'entrée de la grotte et appelle : "Il y a quelqu'un là-dedans ?"
La réponse vient : "Qui c'est ?" Le chef de l'équipe : "La Croix-Rouge".
Untel: "Merci, j'ai déjà donné".

❧ ❧

Möglicherweise hängt es mit einem angeborenen Gefühl der Unsicherheit zusammen, aber wir haben Angst, wir suchen immer wieder nach dem eigenen Ich, oder wir machen uns einfach Sorgen. Meistens machen wir uns Sorgen über das liebe Geld.

Einige Europäer können das besser als andere; beispielsweise die Schotten, die Holländer (deren Land zu flach für Berghöhlen ist), die Galicier im Nordwesten von Spanien, die Galitzianer in Polen und, ausgerechnet, die pontischen Griechen (das sind die, die sich rechter Hand befinden wenn Sie vom Südpol kommen und zum Schwarzen Meer möchten).

Herr Soundso (Schotte, pontischer Grieche, usw.) überlebt einen Flugzeugabsturz auf einem entlegenen Berg. Er hat Hunger, ist erschöpft und findet Zuflucht in einer Höhle. Eine Suchmannschaft vom Roten Kreuz besteigt den Berg, findet den Höhleneingang und ruft "Ist jemand da ?" - "Wer fragt ?", kommt die Antwort. "Das Rote Kreuz", ruft der Führer der Suchmannschaft zurück. "Danke nein", schallt es zurück, "Ich hab' bereits gegeben !"

The situations described in these traditional European jokes are noticeably and appropriately low-tech. But with progress, ships, caves and the like are progressively giving way to space probes, aircraft and such. Here is one example.

The European Union invites applications from astronauts for the first European manned mission to Mars. The first to apply is an Englishman who says he will go for 2 million ECUs, one million for himself and one million for his wife. Next comes a Frenchman, who asks for 3 million ECUs, one million for himself, one million for his wife and one million for his mistress. The final applicant is an Italian who asks for 4 million ECUs. "Why so much?", the project manager asks him. "One million for you, one million for me and two million for that silly Englishman..."

゜゜ ゜

Wat opvalt bij deze traditionele Europese grappen is dat er geen high-tech aan te pas komt. Maar geleidelijk aan moeten schepen, holen en dergelijke plaats maken voor ruimteschepen, vliegtuigen en aanverwanten.

De Europese Unie vroeg astronauten zich kandidaat te stellen voor de eerste bemande Europese ruimtevlucht naar Mars. De eerste kandidaat was een Engelsman, hij vroeg 2 miljoen ecu, één miljoen voor zichzelf en één miljoen voor zijn vrouw. De volgende kandidaat was een Fransman, hij vroeg 3 miljoen ecu: één miljoen voor zichzelf, één miljoen voor zijn vrouw en één miljoen voor zijn maîtresse. De laatste kandidaat was een Italiaan, die 4 miljoen ecu vroeg. "Waarom zo'n hoog bedrag ?" vroeg de projectleider. "Een miljoen voor u, één miljoen voor mij en twee miljoen voor de halvegare Engelsman...".

On aura remarqué que la technique, forcément, intervient peu dans le contexte de ces blagues européennes traditionnelles. Mais, avec l'avancée du progrès, les navires, les grottes et compagnie font progressivement place aux sondes spatiales, aux avions, etc. Voici un exemple.

L'Union européenne invite les astronautes à poser leurs candidatures pour la première mission européenne habitée vers Mars. Le premier candidat est un Anglais, qui dit qu'il est prêt à partir pour 2 millions d'ECU, un million pour lui et un million pour sa femme. Ensuite se présente un Français, qui demande 3 millions d'ECU, un million pour lui, un million pour sa femme et un million pour sa maîtresse. Le dernier candidat est un Italien, qui demande 4 millions d'ECU. "Pourquoi autant ?", lui demande le directeur du projet.
"Un million pour toi, un million pour moi et deux millions pour cet imbécile d'Anglais..."

❧ ❦

Die in traditionelle europäischen Witzen beschriebene Situationen sind sichtlich und angemessenerweise "low-tech". Aber der Fortschritt bringt es mit sich, daß Schiffe, Höhlen und dergleichen zunehmend Dingen wie Raumsonden, Flugzeugen usw. weichen müssen. Es folgt ein Beispiel.

Die Europäische Union nimmt Bewerbungen von Astronauten für den ersten europäischen bemannten Raumflug zum Mars entgegen. Als erster bewirbt sich ein Engländer, der das Wagnis für 2 Mio ECU unternehmen will, eine Million für ihn selbst und eine Million für seine Frau. Dann kommt ein Franzose, der 3 Mio ECU verlangt, nämlich eine Million für sich, eine Million für seine Frau und eine Million für seine Geliebte. Der letzte Bewerber ist Italiener und er möchte 4 Mio ECU. "Warum soviel ?" fragt ihn der Projektleiter.
"Eine Million für Sie, eine Million für mich und zwei Millionen für den albernen Engländer..."

You will notice that triangular jokes, whilst also used amongst neighbours (eg Swedes/Norwegians/Danes and Scots/Welsh/Irish), are often aimed continent-wide at Italians. Think about it a bit and you realise that, far from making fun of the Italians, these jokes acknowledge that Italians are, or at least may be, cleverer than the rest of us. We hate admitting it, but...

In fact, whatever happened to the jokes about the Scotsman, the Welshman and the Irishman?

Three Allied pilots are shot down during the Gulf War: a Frenchman, an Englishman and an Italian. Captured, they are subjected to 'ways of making them talk'. The Frenchman, quite logically not interested in suffering unnecessary pain and disfigurement, talks on the first day. The Englishman, true to his 'stiff-upper-lip' tradition, holds out for a week. The Italian is tortured by his capturers for a month and never talks. Released from captivity, he is debriefed by Allied Intelligence who can't understand how he held out so long. "But 'ow could I talk", he says, "with my 'ands tied be'ind my back?".

❧ ❦

Buren zoals de Zweden, Noren en Denen of de Schotten, mensen uit Wales en de Ieren, maken ook veel grappen over derden, maar overal in Europa moeten de Italianen het ontgelden. Het is een doordenkertje, want op het eerste gezicht lijkt het of het altijd weer de Italianen zijn, die belachelijk gemaakt worden, maar in wezen zijn die grappen een erkenning van het feit dat de Italianen wel eens slimmer zouden kunnen zijn dan wij allemaal samen.

En hoe komt het eigenlijk dat je tegenwoordig geen grappen meer hoort over een Schot, een man uit Wales en een Ier....?

Tijdens de Golfoorlog worden drie geallieerde piloten neergeschoten: een Fransman, een Engelsman en een Italiaan. De krijgsgevangenen krijgen het zwaar te verduren tijdens hun derdegraads verhoor. De Fransman voelt er logischerwijs niets voor om onnodig pijn te lijden en verminking te riskeren en dus vertelt hij de eerste dag alles wat hij weet. De Engelsman, doet de bekende 'stiff-upper-lip' traditie alle eer aan en houdt het een week uit voor hij begint te praten. De Italiaan wordt een maand lang gefolterd, maar laat geen woord los. Na zijn vrijlating wil de Geallieerde Spionagedienst er het fijne van weten, want ze begrijpen niet hoe hij het zolang heeft kunnen volhouden. "Praten ?", zei hij, "met m'n handen op mijn rug zeker ?"

Vous remarquerez que dans toute l'Europe, les blagues triangulaires, bien qu'également utilisées entre voisins (p. ex. Suédois/Norvégiens/Danois ou Ecossais/Gallois/Irlandais), visent souvent les Italiens. Réfléchissez-y un instant et vous vous rendrez compte que bien loin de tourner les Italiens en dérision, ces histoires admettent que les Italiens sont, ou du moins peuvent parfois être, plus futés que tous les autres. Nous n'aimons pas l'admettre, et pourtant...

Et à propos, où sont les blagues sur l'Ecossais, le Gallois et l'Irlandais ?

Pendant la Guerre du Golfe, trois pilotes alliés sont abattus : un Français, un Anglais et un Italien. Ils sont capturés et soumis aux "moyens de les faire parler". Le Français, assez logiquement peu intéressé à souffrir des tourments et des mutilations superflues, parle le premier jour. L'Anglais, fidèle à sa tradition de rigidité, tient le coup pendant une semaine. L'Italien est torturé par ses geôliers pendant un mois et ne parle pas. Relâché, il est interrogé par les services secrets alliés, qui ne comprennent pas comment il a pu tenir aussi longtemps. "Ma, comment tu veux que je parle," dit-il, "avec les mains attachées derrière le dos ?"

※ ⁂

Sie werden schon gemerkt haben, daß Dreieckwitze zwar auch zwischen Nachbarn (z.B. Schweden/Norwegern/Dänen sowie Schotten/Waliser/Iren) üblich sind, aber recht häufig und über den ganzen Kontinent hinweg, die Italiener im Visier haben. Darüber sollte man nachdenken, denn mit diesen Witzen sollen die Italiener ja gar nicht verspottet werden und es geht nur daraus hervor, daß die Italiener schlauer sind, oder zumindest sein könnten, als wir. Wir geben es zwar höchst ungern zu, aber...

Drei Piloten der Alliierten werden im Golfkrieg abgeschossen : ein Franzose, ein Engländer und ein Italiener. Nach ihrer Gefangennahme werden sie "schärfstens" verhört. Der Franzose, an unnötigen Schmerzen und Verunstaltungen logischerweise überhaupt nicht interessiert, sagt alles gleich am ersten Tag. Der Engländer, getreu der Tradition, stets Haltung zu bewahren, kippt erst nach einer Woche um. Der Italiener dagegen wird nach seiner Gefangennahme einen ganzen Monat lang gefoltert, ohne etwas zu sagen. Nach seiner Entlassung aus der Gefangenschaft wird er vom alliierten Nachrichtendienst befragt, denn man möchte wissen, warum er so lange standgehalten hat. "Aber wie hätte ich reden sollen", erklärt er, "mit beiden Händen hinter meinem Rücken gefesselt ?"

Goodness knows where this one came from, but I like to think it's American (it could in fact be Dutch or Belgian, since both countries can, if only occasionally, laugh at themselves, unlike the French).

Quite obviously, it hints at the frugality of the Dutch (we choose our words carefully) and, less obviously, at the anonymity of the Belgians - something that should be of some concern to that country as time goes by.

A trainee pilot is briefed at JFK Airport for his first flight to Brussels. His navigator explains: "You fly due east until you reach a major landmass. That's Europe. The first thing you'll see is rows of freshly washed toilet paper out to dry. That's Holland. Turn 90 degrees to starboard and descend. That's Belgium."

De herkomst van deze grap is in nevelen gehuld, ik houd het op Amerika, maar het zou me niets verbazen als deze grap van Nederlandse of Belgische herkomst is, want die landen kunnen van tijd tot tijd nog wel eens om zichzelf lachen, wat van de Fransen niet gezegd kan worden.

Deze grap verwijst openlijk naar de soberheid van de Nederlanders (en dat is mild uitgedrukt) en in tweede instantie naar het weinig uitgesproken beeld dat men van de Belgen heeft, iets wat dat land toch enige zorg zou moeten baren.

Een piloot in opleiding krijgt op de luchthaven JFK instructies voor zijn eerste vlucht naar Brussel. Zijn navigator geeft hem deze uitleg: "Je blijft doorvliegen tot je bij een heel groot stuk land komt. Dat is Europa. Het eerste wat je ziet zijn lange rijen pas gewassen toiletpapier. Dat is Holland. Negentig graden naar stuurboord en gaan landen. Dan ben je in België."

Dieu sait d'où vient celle-ci, mais j'aimerais qu'elle soit américaine (en fait, elle pourrait être néerlandaise ou belge, étant donné que ces deux pays peuvent, ne serait-ce qu'occasionnellement, rire d'eux-mêmes, au contraire des Français).

A l'évidence, elle fait allusion au sens de l'économie des Néerlandais (je choisis mes mots prudemment) et, de façon moins évidente, à l'anonymat des Belges. Ces derniers devraient d'ailleurs commencer à s'en préoccuper.

A l'aéroport JFK, un élève pilote reçoit ses instructions pour son premier vol sur Bruxelles. Son navigateur explique : "Tu voles tout droit vers l'est jusqu'à ce que tu voies une grande masse de terre. C'est l'Europe. La première chose que tu verras sont des rangées de papier de toilette fraîchement lavées qui sèchent sur des fils. Ça, ce sont les Pays-Bas. Vire de 90° à tribord et descends. Ça, c'est la Belgique."

❦ ❦

Weiß der Himmel wo dieser herkommt, aber mir persönlich wäre es am liebsten, wenn es ein amerikanischer Witz wäre (dabei habe ich den leisen Verdacht, es könnte sich um einen holländischen oder belgischen handeln, denn in beiden Ländern bringen die Leute es manchmal fertig, über sich selbst zu lachen, was bei der Franzosen nicht immer zutrifft).

Offensichtlich geht es dabei um die Sparsamkeit der Holländer (wobei ich mich vorsichtig ausgedrückt habe) und, etwas weniger offensichtlich, um das Nichtbekanntsein der Belgier; letzteres sollte den Einwohnern dieses Landes mit der Zeit doch etwas zu denken geben.

Ein frischgebackener Pilot erhält auf dem JFK-Flughafen die Anweisungen für seien ersten Flug nach Brüssel. Sein Navigator faßt zusammen : "Du fliegst geradeaus in östlichen Richtung bis Du viel Festland siehst. Das ist Europa. Als erstes siehst Du dann frischgewaschenes Klopapier in Reihen zum Trocknen ausgelegt. Das ist Holland. Dann drehst Du 90 Grad nach Steuerbord ab und landest. Das ist Belgien."

The Irish with their whimsical sense of humour, reinforced by a natural talent for saying no good about themselves (look how Irish playwrights portray their fellow-countryfolk!), invite attention from the English and their other European neighbours. You know the joke about the Irish space mission to the sun? Someone objects that they'll get burned up. "For sure we won't", comes the reply, "we'll fly there by night!". That sounds a clever idea. Other jokes, like this one, are plain stupid but can still raise a chuckle.

Two Irishmen, stranded on an iceberg in the North Atlantic, are losing hope of ever being found. Suddenly one of them jumps up. "We're saved!", he shouts, "here comes the Titanic!".

Ieren hebben een nogal typisch gevoel voor humor en beschikken over een natuurtalent om kwaad te spreken van zichzelf (de manier waarop Ierse toneelschrijvers hun landgenoten afschilderen is daar een goed voorbeeld van!). Een karaktertrek die de Engelsen en hun andere buren in Europa opmerkelijk vinden.

Kent u dat verhaal over de Ierse ruimtevlucht naar de zon ? Iemand wees ze erop dat ze dan beslist zouden verbranden.

"Geen sprake van", was het antwoord, "want we vliegen 's nachts !"

Heel snugger, inderdaad. Grappen zoals deze, zijn het toppunt van domheid en toch schiet je in de lach.

Twee Ieren zitten vast op een ijsberg in de Noordatlantische Oceaan en de kans dat ze ooit gevonden worden, slinkt.

Ineens springt één van de twee op en juicht: "We zijn gered, daar heb je de Titanic !".

Les Irlandais, avec leur sens de l'humour insolite, renforcé par un talent naturel pour l'auto-critique (songez à la façon dont les dramaturges irlandais décrivent leurs compatriotes!) suscitent l'attention des Anglais et de leurs autres voisins européens. Vous connaissez celle de la mission spatiale irlandaise vers le soleil? Quelqu'un objecte qu'ils vont griller. "Pour sûr que non," lui réplique-t-on. "On ira pendant la nuit!". Une bonne idée, dirait-on... D'autres blagues, comme celle-ci, sont tout à fait stupides, mais peuvent quand même faire naître un sourire.

Deux Irlandais échoués sur un iceberg de l'Atlantique Nord perdent peu à peu tout espoir d'être retrouvés un jour. Soudain, l'un d'eux se redresse d'un bond. "Nous sommes sauvés!", crie-t-il, "voici le Titanic!".

Die Iren haben einen wunderlichen Sinn für Humor, der vom natürlichen Bedürfnis verstärkt wird, kein gutes Haar an der eigenen Landsleuten zu lassen (beispielhaft dafür ist die Art und Weise, wie irische Dramatiker die Menschen ihrer Heimat schildern!) und werden deshalb gerne zur Zielscheibe der Engländer und anderer europäischer Nachbarn. Kennen Sie den über die irische Raumfahrtmission zur Sonne? Jemand wendet ein, die Raumfahrer würden verbrennen. "Aber nicht doch", kommt die Antwort, "wir fliegen nur nachts!". Das ist doch clever, oder nicht? Andere Witze sind ganz einfach doof, aber leise gelacht wird doch.

Zwei Iren sind auf einem im Nordatlantik schwimmenden Eisberg gestrandet und haben jede Hoffnung verloren, je aufgefunden zu werden. Plötzlich springt einer vor Freude in die Luft. "Wir sind gerettet!", schreit er, "hier kommt die Titanic!".

The Irish have evidently done a good job in self-inflicted character assassination. This is another joke I have heard told against them - although I'm sure that, like so many of these jokes, it has since been adapted to suit other nationalities and may even have originated somewhere else...

A man giving a talk to a multinational audience tells a joke against the Irish (it could be anyone). Someone at the back of the hall jumps up and protests angrily: "I'm Irish!". "OK", says the speaker, "I'll say it again - slowly".

❦ ❦

De Ieren deinzen duidelijk niet terug voor karaktermoord op zichzelf. Dit is nog zo'n grap die ik heb horen vertellen over Ieren. Maar ik ben er zeker van dat men, zoals meestal bij dit soort grappen, er sindsdien al andere nationaliteiten voor heeft ingevuld en het is best mogelijk dat de oorsprong zelfs ergens anders ligt.

Iemand spreekt voor een multinationaal publiek en vertelt een Ieren (of vul zelf maar in)-mop. Een van de toehoorders achter in de zaal springt boos op en roept: "Ik ben een Ier !".

"Goed", antwoordt de spreker, "Ik vertel 'm nog eens, maar dan langzaam".

Manifestement, les Irlandais ont bien réussi à massacrer leur propre image. Voici une autre blague entendue à leur propos - mais je suis sûr que depuis, comme bon nombre de ces blagues, elle a été transposée à d'autres nationalités, et pourrait même trouver son origine ailleurs...

Un homme s'adressant à une audience internationale raconte une blague sur les Irlandais (ou n'importe qui d'autre). Dans le fond de la salle, quelqu'un se lève d'un bond et proteste furieusement : "Je suis Irlandais !". "D'accord", dit l'orateur, "je vais la répéter - lentement".

※ ❧

Die Iren sind ganz große Künstler, wenn es um die Herabwürdigung der eigenen Person und Landsleute geht. Hier ist noch ein Witz, der mir über die Iren erzählt wurde, aber ich bin mir ziemlich sicher, daß er wie so viele andere der gleichen Art, bereits so umgemodelt wurde, daß er auch zu anderen Nationalitäten paßt und möglicherweise seinen Ursprung in einem ganz anderen Teil der Welt hatte...

Ein Mann hält einen Vortrag vor einer multinationalen Zuhörerschaft und erzählt einen Witz über die Iren (oder über andere...). In der letzten Reihe springt jemand auf und protestiert mit lauter Stimme: "Ich bin Ire !". "OK", sagt der Sprecher, "Dann sag ich's noch mal - diesmal langsamer".

The Irish have their own understanding of reality which, as often as not, defies logic. If you're English, your immediate reaction (and your predisposition) is to think they are entirely batty but then, on reflection, you have to conclude that they may have something after all. Like the joke about the Irish weather: "If you can see the mountains, it's about to rain. If you can't see them, it's already raining..."

Here's another Irish anecdote, told as a true story rather than a joke, which has the merit of highlighting this intelligent illogicality of the Irish, something the English would like to have more of themselves.

Waiting for a train in Ireland, an English gentleman remarks loudly and indignantly that the station's three clocks are each showing a different time.

"But", retorts the Irish stationmaster who overhears the comment, "what would be the point of having three of them if they all told the same time?"

※ ❦

Ieren hebben hun eigen benadering van de werkelijkheid, waar doorgaans niet veel logica aan te ontdekken valt. Engelsen gaan ervan uit, en daar komt ook een dosis vooroordeel bij, dat ze compleet geschift zijn, maar als je er wat langer over nadenkt, lijkt er toch wel wat in te zitten. Zoals die grap over het weer in Ierland: " Als je de bergen kunt zien, gaat het binnenkort regenen. Als je ze niet kunt zien, dan regent het al..."

Nog een Ierse anekdote, meer een waar gebeurd verhaal dan een grap, die benadrukt hoe intelligent onlogisch de Ieren kunnen zijn. En de Engelsen zouden daar best wat van op kunnen steken.

Ergens in Ierland staat een Engelse gentleman op de trein te wachten en hij verkondigt op luide en verontwaardigde toon dat de drie klokken op het station elk een verschillende tijd aangeven.

"Maar", reageert de Ierse stationschef op deze opmerking, "wat hebben we aan drie klokken als die allemaal dezelfde tijd aangeven?"

Les Irlandais ont leur propre vision de la réalité qui, le plus souvent, défie toute logique. Si vous êtes Anglais, votre réaction immédiate (et prédisposition) sera de penser qu'ils sont complètement jetés, mais, après réflexion, vous serez obligé de conclure qu'il y a peut-être du vrai dans ce qu'ils disent. C'est comme la blague sur la météo irlandaise : "Si vous pouvez voir les montagnes, c'est qu'il va bientôt pleuvoir. Si vous ne pouvez pas les voir, c'est qu'il pleut déjà..."

Voici une autre anecdote irlandaise, qui passe pour une histoire vraie plutôt que comme une blague, et qui a le mérite de souligner cet intelligent manque de logique des Irlandais, trait de caractère que les Anglais aimeraient intensifier chez eux-mêmes.

Un gentleman anglais qui attend un train en Irlande remarque bruyamment, avec indignation, que les trois horloges de la gare mentionnent toutes une heure différente. "Mais", réplique le chef de gare irlandais, entendant le commentaire, "à quoi cela nous servirait-il d'en avoir trois si elles indiquaient toutes la même heure ?"

🌱 🌿

Die Iren haben einen eigenartigen Wirklichkeitssinn, der ziemlich häufig jeder Logik entbehrt. Als Engländer dürfte Ihre erste Reaktion (und natürliche Veranlagung) sein, daß diese Leute wohl plemplem sind, aber dann denken Sie nach und gelangen zum Schluß, daß doch etwas dran sein muß. Wie beim Witz über das Wetter in Irland: "Wenn man die Berge sieht, regnet es bald. Sieht man sie nicht, dann regnet es bereits..."

Noch eine irische Anekdote, die eher als wahre Geschichte denn als Witz erzählt wird und den Vorteil hat, die intelligente Unlogik der Iren, von der die Engländer eine größere Portion ihr eigen nennen möchten, gebührend zu unterstreichen.

Auf einem Bahnsteig in Irland wartet ein Engländer auf den Zug und äußert sich lautstark und empört zur Tatsache, daß die drei Bahnhofsuhren jede eine andere Zeit angeben. "Aber, aber", sagt ihm der interessiert zuhörende Bahnhofsvorsteher, "was für einen Sinn hätte es, drei von den Dingern zu haben wenn jedes die gleiche Uhrzeit anzeigt ?"

Religion doesn't crop up all that often in European jokes. When it does, it's generally a pretext for making a point about something else. In this case, the 'something else' is the idea that the Irish are an ignorant lot. Whoever thought this one up should know better...

A Roman Catholic Irishman starts a fight with a Jew in the middle of a crowded street. A policeman reaches the scene, breaks up the brawl and asks the Irishman why he started the fight. "Well, he's a Jew and it's the Jews who crucified our Lord", comes the reply. "But that was 2,000 years ago", says the policeman. "I know", replies the Irishman, "but I only found out yesterday".

❧ ❦

In Europese grappen komt het geloof niet bijster vaak ter sprake. En als dat wel het geval is en wordt dan meestal gebruikt op een minder openlijke manier zijn mening ten beste te geven over iets heel anders. Bij deze grap is dat 'iets' de opvatting dat de Ieren een dom volk zouden zijn. De bedenker van deze grap zou beter moeten weten...

Een roomskatholieke Ier zoekt midden in een drukke straat ruzie met een Jood. Er komt een politieagent langs, die de vechtersbazen uit elkaar haalt. En dan vraagt hij de Ier waarom hij wilde vechten.

"Kijk, hij is een Jood en het zijn de Joden die Onze Lieve Heer gekruisigd hebben", krijgt hij ten antwoord. "Maar dat is 2000 jaar geleden", zegt de politieagent. "Dat is ook zo", zegt de Ier, "maar ik weet het pas sinds gisteren".

La religion n'est pas très présente dans les blagues européennes. Le cas échéant, elle est généralement prétexte à insister sur autre chose. Dans ce cas-ci, ce "quelque chose" est l'idée que les Irlandais sont tous des ignorants. L'individu qui a inventé celle-ci ferait mieux de s'informer...

Un catholique irlandais de l'Eglise romaine commence à se battre avec un Juif au milieu d'une rue passante. Un policier arrive sur les lieux, fait cesser la rixe et demande à l'Irlandais pourquoi il a lancé la bagarre. "Eh bien, il est juif, et ce sont les Juifs qui ont crucifié notre Seigneur", lui rétorque-t-on. "Mais c'était il y a 2.000 ans", dit le policier. "Je sais", répond l'Irlandais, "mais je ne l'ai appris qu'hier".

Über die Religion gibt es nicht so viele Witze in Europa. Wenn doch, dann meistens als Vorwand für eine Pointe über ein anderes Thema. In diesem Fall ist das andere Thema die Vorstellung, die Iren seien ein unwissendes Volk. Wer die Geschichte auch erfunden haben mag, hätte es eigentlich besser wissen müssen...

Ein römisch-katholischer Ire fängt mitten in einer belebten Straße heftigen Streit mit einem Juden an. Ein Polizist kommt, trennt die Streithähne und fragt den Iren, warum er den Streit angefangen hat. "Nun, er ist ein Jude und die Juden haben den Herrn gekreuzigt", erhält er als Antwort. "Aber das war doch vor 2000 Jahren", wendet der Polizeibeamte ein. "Ich weiß", antwortet der Ire, "aber ich hab's erst gestern erfahren !".

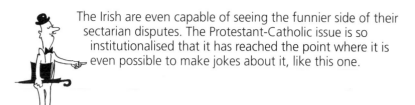

The Irish are even capable of seeing the funnier side of their sectarian disputes. The Protestant-Catholic issue is so institutionalised that it has reached the point where it is even possible to make jokes about it, like this one.

A tourist walks through the no-man's-land between the Protestant and Catholic areas of Belfast, when he is challenged by a masked gunman: "Are you Protestant or Catholic?". "I'm neither", says the tourist, "I'm Jewish". "OK", says the gunman, undeterred, "are you a Protestant or a Catholic Jew?".

❧ ❧

De Ieren bezitten zelfs het vermogen om hun sektarische twisten van de grappige kant te bekijken. De tegenstellingen tussen de Katholieken en de Protestanten zijn dermate deel gaan uitmaken van het dagelijks leven dat het nu zover is dat men er zelfs grappen over kan maken, zoals deze.

Een toerist loopt door het niemandsland tussen het Protestantse en het Katholieke deel van Belfast en krijgt te maken met een gemaskerde man die hem onder bedreiging met een wapen vraagt: "Protestant of Katholiek ?". "Geen van beide", antwoordt de toerist, "Ik ben Joods". "Ja, maar", blijft de man met het wapen volhouden, "een protestantse of een katholieke Jood ?".

Les Irlandais sont même capables de voir le côté comique de leurs querelles sectaires. Le conflit entre catholiques et protestants est tellement institutionnalisé qu'on en est au point de pouvoir inventer des blagues à cè sujet, comme celle-ci.

Un touriste traverse le no man's land qui s'étend entre les zones catholique et protestante de Belfast, lorsqu'il est interpellé par un bandit armé : "Etes-vous catholique ou protestant ?". "Ni l'un ni l'autre", dit le touriste, "je suis juif". "OK", dit le bandit, sans sourciller, "juif catholique ou protestant ?".

🌱 🐛

Die Iren können selbst die komische Seite ihrer konfessionellen Streitereien erkennen. Der Streit zwischen Protestantismus und Katholizismus ist so weitgehend zur heiligen Kuh geworden, daß man sogar Witze darüber reißen kann, so wie diesen hier.

Ein Tourist spaziert im Niemandsland zwischen den protestantischen und den katholischen Vierteln in Belfast herum und wird von einem Maskierten mit Waffe angehalten und verhört: "Bist Du Protestant oder Katholik ?". "Nichts von beiden", antwortet der Tourist, "Ich bin Jude". "OK", sagt der Bewaffnete unverzagt, "bist Du ein protestantischer oder ein katholischer Jude ?".

In days before Political Correctness US-style, many American jokes were about European immigrants, Polish and Irish immigrants in particular. Many of these jokes were indeed rather abusive. Here's a joke which you may consider either convoluted or incomprehensible.

Shaun Ferguson is a German-speaking Polish immigrant to the US. Somebody asks him why he has a Scots name.
"Well, it's like this", he explains. "I have a very difficult Polish name and, when I emigrate to the United States, I forget all about it. This immigration officer on Ellis Island, he ask me to give my old name. I don't remember. I put my hand to my head and cry "Aie, schon vergessen!".

❦ ❧

In de tijd voor politiek correct zijn in zwang raakte in Amerika, gingen veel Amerikaanse grappen over Europese immigranten en dan vooral over Poolse en Ierse immigranten. Veel van die grappen waren tamelijk grof.

Dit is een grap die naar gelang óf nogal gezocht óf onbegrijpelijk gevonden wordt.

Shaun Ferguson is een duitssprekende Pool die naar Amerika geëmigreerd is. Iemand vraagt hem hoe hij aan zijn Schotse naam komt.
"Kijk, dat zit zo", zegt hij. "Ik heb een hele moeilijke Poolse naam en toen ik naar de Verenigde Staten geëmigreerd ben, was ik die naam compleet vergeten. De man van de immigratiedienst op Ellis Island vroeg me om mijn oude naam op te geven. Ik vergeten. Ik slaan voor het hoofd en roepen "Aie, schon vergessen !".

A l'époque où l'on ne parlait pas encore du style américain "politiquement correct", beaucoup de blagues américaines portaient sur les immigrants européens, notamment les Polonais et les Irlandais. Nombre de ces blagues étaient, en effet, assez mordantes. Voici une plaisanterie que vous jugerez peut-être obscure ou incompréhensible.

Shaun Ferguson est un Polonais germanophone immigré aux USA. Quelqu'un lui demande pourquoi il a un nom écossais. "Eh bien", explique-t-il, "mon nom polonais, très compliqué. Quand je émigrer aux Etats-Unis, je oublier complètement le nom. Le officier de immigration à Ellis Island me demander mon ancien nom. Je pas me rappeler. Je mettre ma main à ma front et crier : "Aie, schon vergessen !".

❦ ❧

In den Tagen, ehe die "politische Korrektheit" nach Art der USA erfunden war, handelten viele amerikanische Witze von europäischen Einwanderern, insbesondere von polnischen und irischen Immigranten. Viele dieser Witze waren ziemlich beleidigend. Hier ist ein Witz, den Sie entweder als höchst gewunden oder als unverständlich bewerten dürften.

Shaun Ferguson ist ein deutschsprachiger polnischer Einwanderer in den USA. Jemand fragt ihn nach seinem schottischen Namen und er erklärt folgendes: "Nun ja, das ist so, Ich habe einen sehr komplizierten polnischen Namen und als ich in die Vereinigte Staaten ausgewandert war, ist er mir entfallen. Der Beamte der Einwanderungsbehörde auf Ellis Island fragte mich nach meinem Namen, aber den hatte ich vergessen. Ich griff mir an den Kopf und jammerte: "Aii, schon vergessen !".

This one may well have started off in the States - after all there are a lot of people of Italian descent in the USA. Like many other jokes, it has the Texans as the butt, yet it tells us as much about the fatalism of the Italians (even if the trains did run on time there for a while).

A Texan, on holiday in Italy, is trying to impress his host. He brags about everything imaginable - the size of the vegetables, the size of the cattle, the size of the estates and finally, since his listener is still totally unimpressed, the size of the state. "You know", he says, "you can get on a train and, 24 hours later, you're still in Texas". "You know", replies the Italian, "we have that problem all the time!"

❧ ❧

Misschien vindt deze grap zijn oorsprong wel in de Verenigde Staten, er wonen immers heel veel mensen van Italiaanse origine in VS. Zoals bij grappen vaak het geval is, zijn de Texanen het mikpunt, maar is de inhoud even veelzeggend over het fatalisme van de Italianen (want dat van die treinen die op tijd liepen, dat was immers maar tijdelijk...).

Een Texaan, die op vakantie is in Italië, probeert zijn gastheer te imponeren. Je kunt het zo gek niet bedenken of hij schept erover op: hoe groot de groente wel niet is en de kuddes, hoe uitgestrekt de landerijen zijn en aangezien zijn gehoor nog steeds niet erg onder de indruk is, over hoe groot de staat Texas wel niet is.

"Weet u", zegt hij, als je met de trein rijdt ben je vierentwintig uur later nog steeds in Texas". "Zeg", antwoordt de Italiaan, "daar hebben wij hier nu ook de hele tijd last van !"

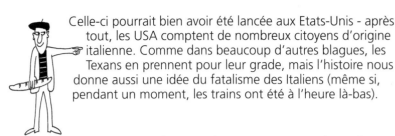

Celle-ci pourrait bien avoir été lancée aux Etats-Unis - après tout, les USA comptent de nombreux citoyens d'origine italienne. Comme dans beaucoup d'autres blagues, les Texans en prennent pour leur grade, mais l'histoire nous donne aussi une idée du fatalisme des Italiens (même si, pendant un moment, les trains ont été à l'heure là-bas).

Un Texan en vacances en Italie tente d'impressionner son hôte. Il se vante de tout et de n'importe quoi - la taille des légumes, du bétail, des propriétés et finalement, comme son auditeur ne semble pas se laisser démonter, de l'étendue de son Etat. "Vous savez", dit-il, "vous pouvez monter dans un train et, 24 heures plus tard, vous êtes toujours au Texas." "Vous savez", réplique l'Italien, "nous avons ce problème tout le temps !"

❧ ❦

Es kann schon sein, daß dieser Witz in den USA entstanden ist, denn Menschen italienischer Abstammung gibt es ja dort in rauhen Mengen. Wie recht viele Witze dort, machen sie die Texaner zwar zur Zielscheibe des Spottes, aber auch der Fatalismus der Italiener kommt darin nicht zu kurz (auch wenn die Züge dort eine gewisse Zeitlang pünktlich fuhren).

Ein Texaner macht Urlaub in Italien und befleißigt sich, seinen Gastgeber zu beeindrucken. Er prahlt unaufhörlich mit allem und jenem. Von der Größe des Gemüses, der Rinder, der Farmen, bis schließlich hin zur Größe von Texas, weil sein Gastgeber sich völlig unbeeindruckt zeigt. "Wissen Sie," sagt er, "Sie steigen in den Zug und 24 Stunden später sind Sie immer noch in Texas".

"Ach wissen Sie," antwortet der Italiener, "das Problem kennen wir auch hier !"

Not fair on Sicilians, but who cares anyway - certainly not the Sicilians I've told this joke to. It's an intelligent joke because it contains a number of (partly false) perceptions of the people it refers to: Sicilians often are small, some of them may have mother-fixations (don't we all?), but they are certainly not lazy. Not the ones we've met, at any rate.

Q: *Why are Sicilians so small?*

A: *Because, when they were little, their mothers told them they would have to work when they grew up.*

❦ ❧

Het getuigt niet bepaald van eerlijkheid tegenover de Sicilianen, maar wat kan ons dat schelen...Dat gold in ieder geval voor de Sicilianen die ik deze grap verteld heb. Deze grap getuigt van intelligentie want er is sprake van een reeks (soms misplaatste) opvattingen over de mensen in kwestie: Sicilianen zijn vaak klein van stuk, hebben soms een uitgesproken moederbinding (en wie niet uiteindelijk), maar lui zijn ze beslist niet. Degenen die ik ontmoet heb ten minste niet.

Vraag : Waarom zijn alle Sicilianen zo klein ?

Antwoord : Omdat toen ze klein waren, hun moeder altijd zei, dat als ze groot waren, er gewerkt moest worden.

Méchante pour les Siciliens, mais après tout, qui s'en fait ?
Certainement pas les Siciliens auxquels je l'ai racontée.
C'est une histoire intelligente parce qu'elle contient
plusieurs manières (partiellement erronées) de percevoir les
personnes auxquelles elle fait référence : les Siciliens sont
souvent de petite taille, certains d'entre eux ont peut-être des
fixations maternelles (n'en avons-nous pas tous ?), mais ils ne
sont certainement pas fainéants. Pas ceux que j'ai
rencontrés, tout au moins.

Q : Pourquoi les Siciliens sont-ils tellement petits ?

R : Parce que, quand ils étaient petits, leur "mamma" leur a dit qu'ils
devraient travailler quand ils seraient grands.

Fair den Sizilianern gegenüber ist dieser Witz ja nicht,
aber wen kümmert das schon, am allerwenigsten die
Sizilianer selbst, denen ich ihn erzählt habe. Es handelt
sich um einen intelligenten Witz, weil er eine Reihe
von (zum Teil falschen) Wahrnehmungen über die
betroffenen Menschen zum Gegenstand hat, denn
Sizilianer sind häufig kleinwüchsig, manche mögen auch
starke Mutterbindungen haben (wer hätte die nicht ?),
aber faul sind sie bestimmt nicht. Zumindest nicht
diejenigen, denen wir begegnet sind.

Frage: Warum sind Sizilianer so klein ?

Antwort: Weil Ihre Mütter ihnen als Kinder erzählen, sie müßten
arbeiten, wenn sie groß geworden sind.

Some European cultures excel in their wit without even trying to be funny. The best are the Spanish who, over the centuries, have amassed a treasure-chest of folk wisdom in words. Here are two of the best: they happen to refer to wives and mothers-in-law, a subject that used to be close to the heart of many European males, not least the British.

If your wife tells you to throw yourself out of the window, pray god it's a low one.

If I saw my mother-in-law sitting on a wasps' nest, I would tell her, very slowly, how much I love her.

❧ ❦

Sommige Europese culturen munten uit in sprankelende humor zonder dat ze daar speciaal moeite voor doen. Dat geldt in het bijzonder voor de Spanjaarden, die in de loop der tijden een ware schat aan volkswijsheden hebben verzameld. Twee goede voorbeelden hiervan gaan over echtgenotes en schoonmoeders, een onderwerp dat veel Europese mannen, en de Britten in het bijzonder, lange tijd zeer nauw aan het hart gelegen heeft.

"Als je vrouw zegt dat je uit het raam moet springen, is het te hopen dat het niet te hoog is."

"Als ik zie dat mijn schoonmoeder in een wespennest gaat zitten, lijkt me dat het goede moment om haar heel omstandig te vertellen hoeveel ik van haar houd."

Certaines cultures européennes excellent dans la finesse sans même tenter d'être amusantes. Les meilleurs du genre sont les Espagnols. Au cours des siècles, ils ont amassé un trésor de sagesse populaire en mots. En voici deux des meilleurs. Il se fait qu'ils concernent les épouses et les belles-mères, un sujet jadis cher au coeur de beaucoup d'Européens de sexe masculin, notamment des Britanniques.

Si votre femme vous dit de vous jeter par la fenêtre, priez pour qu'elle soit basse.

Si je voyais ma belle-mère assise sur un nid de guêpes, je lui dirais très lentement combien je l'aime.

୫ ୮

Einige europäische Kulturen zeichnen sich ganz besonders durch ihren Geist aus, wobei sie nicht einmal versuchen, witzig zu sein. Am besten sind in dieser Beziehung die Spanier, die im Laufe der Jahrhunderte einen Schatz an Volksweisheiten zusammengetragen haben.

Hier folgen zwei der besten, die sich zufällig auf Ehefrauen und Schwiegermütter beziehen, ein Thema, das vielen europäischen Ehemännern am Herzen liegt, vor allem auch den Engländern.

Wenn Deine Frau Dir sagt, Du sollst aus dem Fenster springen, dann bete zu Gott, daß es nicht allzu hoch gelegen ist.

Wenn ich sehen würde, daß meine Schwiegermutter auf einem Wespennest sitzt, dann würde ich ihr sagen, wie sehr ich sie mag, aber sehr langsam."

Another gem of Spanish folk wisdom is 'God gives nuts to the toothless'. But one of the best Spanish jokes I know is a genuine conversation overheard by a British-Dutch couple at a poolside party on the Costa del Sol. It tells you something about the Spanish ability to be unfazed.

First Spaniard: "All Brasilians are tarts or football players."
Second Spaniard: "My wife is Brasilian."
First Spaniard: "Which team does she play for?"

❦ ❦

Nog een juweeltje van Spaanse volkswijsheid: 'God overlaadt de tandelozen met noten'. Maar een van de beste Spaanse grappen die ik ken, is dit gesprek dat een Brits-Nederlands echtpaar heus gehoord heeft tijdens een party bij het zwembad ergens langs de Costa del Sol. Waar maar weer eens uit blijkt dat de Spanjaarden niet voor één gat vangen zijn.

Zegt de ene Spanjaard tegen de andere: "In Brazilië heb je alleen sloeries en voetballers".
Zegt de andere Spanjaard: "Mijn vrouw komt uit Brazilië."
Zegt die andere Spanjaard weer: "O, ja, en voor welke club speelt ze ?"

Autre petit bijou de la sagesse populaire espagnole : "Dieu donne des noix aux édentés". Mais l'une des meilleures blagues espagnoles que je connaisse est une conversation réellement entendue par un couple britannico-néerlandais lors d'une réception au bord d'une piscine de la Costa del Sol. Elle vous donne une idée du sang-froid espagnol.

Premier Espagnol: *"Tous les Brésiliens sont des grues ou des joueurs de football."*

Second Espagnol: *"Ma femme est brésilienne."*

Premier Espagnol: *" Elle joue dans quelle équipe ?"*

❦ ❧

Eine Perle spanischer Volksweisheit ist der Satz "Gott gibt den Zahnlosen die dicksten Eier". Aber es geht hier um ein tatsächlich stattgefundenes Gespräch, das von einem britisch/holländischen Paar auf einer Party am Swimming Pool an der Costa del Sol mitgehört wurde. Betont wird die Fähigkeit der Spanier, sich nicht aus der Fassung bringen zu lassen.

"Aus Brasilien kommen nur Flittchen oder Fußballspieler", behauptet der erste Spanier.

Zweiter Spanier :" Meine Frau ist Brasilianerin !"

Erster Spanier :" In welcher Mannschaft spielt sie ?"

Along with the Galicians, it is the Catalans in Spain who have the reputation of being dour, tight-fisted and, of course, successful. Here is the kind of joke the other Spaniards - Castilians, Basques, Estremadurans, Valencians, Andalusians, whatever - tell about the Catalans (they generally talk about 'Jordi' in this kind of joke).

Jordi, mourning the loss of his wife, visits the offices of his local newspaper to arrange an announcement in the obituaries section. "What do you want to say?", asks the clerk. "Maria's dead", replies the distraught Jordi. "But you can have up to ten words for the same price", says the clerk. "OK", says Jordi, "how about adding 'second-hand SEAT for sale'?".

❦ ❧

Net als de Galiciërs hebben de Catalanen in Spanje de reputatie stug, gierig te zijn en, hoe kan het anders, succes in zaken te hebben. Dit is het soort grappen dat andere Spanjaarden – Castilianen, Basken, Estremadorezen, Valencianen, Andalusiërs, noem maar op – vertellen over de Catalanen (die dan meestal 'Jordi' heten).

Jordi rouwt om zijn overleden vrouw en gaat naar de plaatselijke krant om een overlijdensbericht op te geven. "Wat wilt u erin zetten ?", vraagt de man achter de balie. "Maria is dood", antwoordt de intrieste Jordi. "Maar voor die prijs hebt u recht op tien woorden ", zegt de man achter de balie. "O, zet er dan maar bij 'tweedehands SEAT te koop'".

En Espagne, les Catalans, tout comme les Galiciens, ont la réputation d'être austères, radins et, bien sûr, prospères. Voici le genre de blague que les autres Espagnols - de Castille, du Pays Basque, d'Estrémadure, de Valence, d'Andalousie, etc. - racontent sur les Catalans (dans ce genre de plaisanterie, ils parlent généralement de "Jordi").

Jordi, qui vient de perdre sa femme, se rend aux bureaux du journal local pour faire passer une annonce dans la rubrique mortuaire. "Que voulez-vous écrire ?" demande l'employé. "Maria est morte", répond Jordi, éperdu. "Mais, pour le même prix, vous pouvez insérer jusqu'à dix mots", dit l'employé. "D'accord", dit Jordi, "si on ajoutait "SEAT de seconde main à vendre" ?".

❧ ❧

Zusammen mit den Galiciern stehen die Katalanen in Spanien im Ruf, besonders mürrisch, knickerig und, natürlich, erfolgreich zu sein. Hier ist die Art von Witz, den die anderen Spanier - Kastilier, Basken, Estremaduranier, Valencianer, Andalusier usw... - über die Katalanen erzählen (im allgemeinen tritt ein "Jordi" in solchen Witzen auf).

Jordi trauert um seine verstorbene Frau und sucht das Büro der Lokalzeitung auf, um eine Todesanzeige aufnehmen zu lassen. "Was möchten Sie sagen ?" fragt die Angestellte. "Maria ist tot", antwortet der betrübte Jordi. "Aber zum gleichen Preis können Sie zehn Wörter drucken lassen", erklärt die Angestellte. "OK", sagt Jordi, "wie wär's wenn ich 'gebrauchter SEAT zu verkaufen' hinzufügen würde ?".

This joke, despite initial appearances, is told by Norwegians at the expense of Swedes. But it can be told by Swedes at the expense of Norwegians (say 'Swedish' when it says 'Norwegian' and vice versa). It can also be told by Swedes about Danes, by Danes about Swedes, and so on *ad infinitum*. The fact is, it's quite clever.

Put a question to a sample of Norwegian citizens and you will get two per cent who say 'yes', two percent say 'no' and ninety-six per cent say 'don't know'. Put the same question to a Swedish sample and you will get two per cent who say 'yes', two per cent say 'no', two per cent say 'don't know' and ninety-four per cent say 'we didn't understand the question'.

❧ ☙

Hoewel men dat op het eerste gezicht niet zou zeggen, is dit een grap over de Zweden die in Noorwegen opgeld doet. Maar omgekeerd is deze grap even goed van toepassing. En de Zweden vertellen dezelfde grap dan weer over de Denen en de Denen over de Zweden, kortom...

Maar ondanks dat, toch veelzeggend.

Wanneer men een aantal Noren een vraag stelt, antwoordt 2 procent met 'ja', nog eens 2 procent met 'nee' en de resterende 96 procent 'ik weet het niet'. Wanneer men dezelfde vraag aan een aantal Zweden voorlegt, antwoordt 2 procent met 'ja', 2 procent met 'nee', 2 procent met 'ik weet het niet' en 94 procent met 'we begrijpen de vraag niet'.

Contrairement à la première apparence, ce sont les Norvégiens qui racontent cette histoire sur les Suédois. Mais elle peut également être racontée par les Suédois aux dépens des Norvégiens (il suffit de remplacer "Norvégien" par "Suédois" et vice-versa). Les Suédois la racontent sur les Danois, les Danois sur les Suédois... il existe une infinité de combinaisons. Normal, c'est une histoire intelligente.

Posez une question à un échantillon de citoyens norvégiens;
2 % diront "oui", 2 % diront "non" et 96 % diront "je ne sais pas".
Posez la même question à un échantillon de citoyens suédois;
2 % diront "oui", 2 % diront "non", 2 % diront "je ne sais pas", et 94 % diront "nous n'avons pas compris la question."

❦ ❧

Dieser Witz wird, trotz des anfänglichen Eindrucks, von den Norwegern auf Kosten der Schweden erzählt. Es geht aber auch umgekehrt, denn man braucht nur "schwedisch" für "norwegisch" und umgekehrt einzusetzen. Er kann - und wird - auch von Schweden über Dänen, von diesen über Schweden, und so weiter ad infinitum erzählt. Er ist nun mal ziemlich clever.

Wenn man einer Durchschnittsgruppe norwegischer Bürger eine Frage stellt, sagen zwei Prozent 'Ja', zwei Prozent 'Nein' und sechsundneunzig Prozent 'Weiß nicht".

Stellt man die gleiche Frage einer schwedischen Gruppe, bekommt man zwei Prozent 'Ja', zwei Prozent 'Nein', zwei Prozent 'Weiß nicht' und vierundneunzig Prozent sagen "Wir haben die Frage nicht verstanden".

The great merit of the last joke is that it's two-sided: anybody can arrange to have the last laugh. Most ethnic jokes don't have that degree of versatility and end up with someone having a bad taste in the mouth. Yet they often have a wry humour, often a sense of good-natured ridicule, like this Nordic pair (the Swedes and Norwegians have nationalised industries turning out jokes at one another's expense).

When there's a lightning flash in Norway, people come out into the rain to have their photos taken. **(Swedish joke)**

It takes 1001 Swedes to change a lightbulb - one to hold the bulb and one thousand to turn the world anticlockwise. **(Norwegian joke)**

❧ ❦

Het goedaardige van de vorige grap is dat je hem kunt aanpassen aan de omstandigheden en naar believen kunt omdraaien. De meeste op volksaard gebaseerde grappen laten dat niet toe en blijft er bij sommigen dus altijd een wrange nasmaak achter. Vaak getuigen ze ook van een soort droge humor, die zwakheden op de hak neemt zonder verdere bijbedoelingen. Als voorbeeld deze twee uit het Hoge Noorden waar Zweden en Noren grappen ten beste geven over elkaars genationaliseerde bedrijven.

Bij een bliksemflits gaan de Noren buiten staan om op de foto te komen. **(een Zweedse grap)**

Er zijn 1001 Zweden nodig om een lamp te verwisselen: één houdt de lamp vast en de andere duizend om de aarde de verkeerde kant op te draaien. **(een Noorse grap)**

Le grand mérite de l'histoire qui précède est son caractère à double tranchant : tout le monde peut la tourner de manière à rire le dernier. La plupart des blagues ethniques n'ont pas ce degré de flexibilité; elles finissent toujours par laisser un goût amer chez quelqu'un. Cependant, elles témoignent souvent d'un humour grimaçant, ou d'un sens du ridicule bon enfant, comme cette paire de blagues nordique (chez les Suédois et les Norvégiens, produire des blagues aux dépens les uns des autres est une industrie nationale).

Lorsqu'il y a un éclair d'orage en Norvège, les gens sortent dans la pluie pour être sur la photo. **(blague suédoise)**

Il faut 1.001 Suédois pour changer une ampoule - un pour tenir l'ampoule et mille pour faire tourner la Terre dans le sens contraire des aiguilles d'une montre. **(blague norvégienne)**

❦ ❧

Das große Verdienst des letzterzählten Witzes ist, daß er zweischneidig sein kann : jeder kann ihn so ummodeln, daß er die Lacher auf seiner Seite hat. Den meisten ethnischen Witze fehlt diese Anpassungsfähigkeit und es bleibt wie ein schlechter Geschmack im Mund. Häufig bringen sie jedoch einen trockenen Humor und einen Sinn für wohlwollende Lächerlichkeit zum Ausdruck, so wie die folgenden beiden skandinavischen Witze (die Schweden und die Norweger haben verstaatlichte Fabriken, in denen Witze auf Kosten der Nachbarn hergestellt werden).

Wenn es in Norwegen blitzt, dann stellen die Leute sich im Regen auf, um sich fotografieren zu lassen. **(schwedischer Witz)**

Man braucht 1001 Schweden, um eine Glühlampe auszuwechseln - einer hält die Lampe und eintausend drehen die Weltkugel im entgegengesetzten Uhrzeigersinn. **(norwegischer Witz)**

The mutual joking between Swedes and Norwegians is a rich tradition, challenging the countries' reputation for dourness with other Europeans. Despite the fact that the Norwegians were forced into a shotgun marriage with the Swedes from 1814 to 1905, there is an underlying spirit of goodwill which makes such jokes possible. Here's another Swedish one:

An escaped criminal from a Swedish jail is believed to have crossed the frontier into Norway. The Swedish police send identity photos - left profile, full face and right profile.

A couple of weeks later, the reply comes back: "We have identified the man on the left and the one on the right, but we are still looking for the one in the middle".

❧ ❦

Er bestaat een rijke traditie van grappen die de Zweden en de Noren over elkaar vertellen, in weerwil van de stugheid die de bewoners van deze landen door andere Europeanen wordt toegedicht. Ondanks het feit dat de Noren van 1814 tot 1905 door de Zweden tot een huwelijk gedwongen werden, bestaat er onderling een welwillendheid de ruimte laat voor grappen over en weer. Deze komt van de Zweden:

Er is een misdadiger ontsnapt uit een Zweedse gevangenis en men vermoedt dat hij over de Noorse grens gevlucht is. De Zweedse politie stuurt de nodige foto's om hem te kunnen identificeren: linker profiel, portret, rechter profiel.

Een paar weken later komt er antwoord: "De man links hebben we kunnen identificeren en die aan de rechterkant ook, maar van die in het midden is er nog steeds geen spoor".

Les blagues circulant chez les Suédois à propos des Norvégiens et vice-versa sont le fruit d'une riche tradition, qui contredit la réputation d'austérité de ces pays auprès des autres Européens. En dépit du mariage forcé des Norvégiens avec les Suédois de 1814 à 1905, il y a, en filigrane, un esprit de bienveillance permettant des blagues de ce type. Voici une autre Suédoise :

Un délinquant échappé d'une prison suédoise aurait franchi la frontière norvégienne. La police suédoise envoie des photos d'identité - profil gauche, portrait de face et profil droit.

Quelques semaines plus tard arrive la réponse : "Nous avons identifié l'individu de gauche et celui de droite, mais nous recherchons toujours celui du milieu".

❦ ❧

Das gegenseitige Witzereißen zwischen Schweden und Norwegern hat Tradition und lockert in etwa den Ruf der Verdrießlichkeit, in dem beide bei den anderen Europäern stehen. Trotz der Tatsache, daß die Norweger in der Zeit von 1814 bis 1905 in einer Mußehe mit den Schweden leben mußten, besteht untergründig ein Geist des guten Willens, der Witze wie den folgenden möglich machen. Noch ein schwedischer Witz:

Man glaubt, daß ein aus dem Gefängnis in Schweden entflohener Sträfling die Grenze nach Norwegen überschritten hat. Die schwedische Polizei schickt Kennfotos - linkes Profil, von vorne, rechtes Profil.

Zwei Wochen später kommt die Antwort: "Wir haben den Mann rechts und links identifiziert, aber den in der Mitte suchen wir noch".

Here's another Nordic joke, which also tells you something about what these people think of one another. Being a three-sided joke, it doesn't take sides and treats all three parties with equal (dis)respect. It also contains three grains of truth.

A group of Nordics - two Danes, two Norwegians and two Swedes - are rescued by an international team after being stranded for years on a desert island. Brought back to civilisation, they are interviewed by the media who want to know how they got on together. It turns out thet the Danes started a trading post, the Norwegians quarrelled all the time with everybody else, and the two Swedes were still waiting to be introduced.

❧ ❧

Nog een grap uit het Hoge Noorden, die ook aangeeft hoe de mensen daar over elkaar denken. Het gaat om drie groepen van twee, dus wordt er geen partij gekozen en krijgen ze er alle drie van langs. Bovendien bevat de grap drie kernen van waarheid.

Een groep Scandinaviërs bestaand uit twee Denen, twee Noren en twee Zweden, wordt na jaren op een onbewoond eiland, ontdekt door een internationaal reddingsteam. Terug in de beschaving wordt ze bij vraaggesprekken in de media gevraagd of ze het met elkaar konden vinden. En zo bleek dat de Denen een handeltje hadden opgezet, de Noren voortdurend ruzie hadden met iedereen en dat de twee Zweden hadden zitten wachten tot iemand ze aan elkaar voorstelde.

Voici une autre blague nordique qui, elle aussi, fournit quelques indications sur l'opinion de ces peuples vis-à-vis les uns des autres. Etant trilatérale, elle est impartiale et traite les trois protagonistes avec égal (ir)respect. Elle a aussi trois accents de vérité.

Un groupe de Nordiques (deux Danois, deux Norvégiens et deux Suédois) échoués depuis des années sur une île déserte est sauvé par une équipe internationale. Ramenés à la civilisation, ils sont interviewés par les médias qui veulent savoir quels étaient leurs rapports mutuels. Il apparaît que les Danois ont créé un comptoir commercial, que les Norvégiens ont passé tout leur temps à se disputer avec tout le monde, et que les deux Suédois attendaient toujours d'être présentés.

❦ ❦

Noch ein Witz aus dem Norden, aus dem hervorgeht, was diese Leute voneinander halten. Als Dreieckswitz bleibt er neutral und behandelt die drei Parteien mit gleichem Respekt bzw. gleicher Respektlosigkeit.

Eine Gruppe Skandinavier - zwei Dänen, zwei Norweger und zwei Schweden - wird nach langen Jahren auf einer einsamen Insel von einem internationalen Team gerettet. Nachdem die Geretteten wieder unter Menschen sind, werden sie von Journalisten gefragt, wie sie so miteinander ausgekommen sind. Wie sich herausstellt, eröffneten die Dänen ein Handelskontor, die Norweger stritten sich dauernd mit allen herum und die beiden Schweden warteten noch immer darauf, den anderen vorgestellt zu werden.

The joke against oneself is the one that few of us have the courage to tell. The Finns, as in so many other things, are an exception. This joke is not necessarily a comment on Finnish fondness for alcohol - although a police check one recent beautiful, long Finnish summer evening showed that 70% of those interviewed were drunk in charge of their boats. It is really a comment on the Finns' reluctance to speak without reason. Other Europeans could learn from that.

Two old Finnish friends meet up for a drink after a long-time-no-see. There is a protracted but comfortable silence, which lasts some ten minutes. Then one of the Finns looks up and says: "Well, how are you Matti?" To which Matti replies: "Look, did we come here to talk or to drink?".

❦ ❦

Een uiterst sociaalvoelende grap, maar de meesten van ons hebben er de moed niet toe. Net als in veel andere opzichten vormen de Finnen op dit punt een uitzondering. Deze grap verwijst niet zo zeer naar de liefde van de Finnen voor sterke drank, hoewel politiecontrole op een van die lange Finse zomeravonden onlangs uitwees dat 70% van de bootbestuurders dronken was. Wat hier bedoeld wordt, is dat Finnen er het zwijgen toe doen wanneer ze niets te zeggen hebben. Veel andere Europeanen zouden daar hun voordeel mee kunnen doen.

Twee Finnen gaan samen iets drinken, het zijn oude vrienden die elkaar lang niet gezien hebben. Er heerst een prettige, ongedwongen stilte die wel tien minuten duurt. Dan kijkt een van de Finnen op en zegt: "vertel eens, Matti, hoe is 't met je ?" En de reactie van Matti is: "Zeg, kwamen we om te praten of om te drinken ?".

Voici le type d'histoire qui sert le mieux le bien public, mais que peu d'entre nous ont le courage de raconter. Comme pour tant d'autres choses, les Finnois font exception. L'histoire n'est pas nécessairement un commentaire sur le penchant des Finnois pour l'alcool - bien qu'un contrôle de police mené récemment un beau et long soir d'été a montré que 70 % des personnes interrogées étaient saoûles aux commandes de leur bateau. En fait, cette blague illustre la répugnance des Finnois à parler sans raison. D'autres Européens feraient bien de suivre leur exemple.

Après une longue séparation, deux vieux copains finnois se retrouvent pour prendre un verre. Il y a un silence prolongé mais agréable, qui dure près de dix minutes. Puis, l'un des Finnois regarde son ami et demande : "Alors Matti, comment ça va ?" Et Matti de répondre : "On est venu ici pour boire ou pour causer ?"

※ ❦

Es geht hier um die gemeinnützigsten Witze überhaupt, aber nur wenige Menschen bringen den Mut auf, sie zu erzählen. Die Finnen zählen dabei, wie in so manch anderer Hinsicht, zu den rühmlichen Ausnahmen. Der Witz handelt nicht unbedingt vom Hang der Finnen zu alkoholischen Getränken - obwohl sich jüngst, an einem herrlich langen Sommerabend in Finnland, bei einer polizeilichen Kontrolle ergab, daß 70 % der Befragten im Zustand der Trunkenheit ihr Boot steuerten. Eigentlich wird der Widerwille der Finnen gezeigt, ohne guten Grund gesprächig zu werden. Andere Europäer könnten sich daran ein Beispiel nehmen.

Zwei alte finnische Freunde treffen sich nach längerer Zeit zu einem Bier. Schweigend aber gemütlich sitzen sie einander etwa zehn Minuten gegenüber. Dann schaut einer der beiden auf und fragt : "Nun, Matti, wie geht's ?" Und Matti antwortet vorwurfsvoll : "Hör' mal, sind wir hier um zu plaudern oder um zu trinken ?"

In fact, the Finns are what the experts call 'binge drinkers'. They can go dry for weeks on end and, then, all of a sudden hit the bottle. Again, the experts say it goes back - not all that long ago - to the time when all Finns worked on the land. From one week to the other, they had little social contact and no opportunity to let their hair down - until market day when, having sold their produce, they also had a bit of money to spare. No wonder the Finns seem an introvert lot, as this joke implies.

Three businessmen - a German, an Italian and a Finn - go on safari when a huge elephant ambles out of the bush. The German looks at the animal and thinks: "What a powerful beast, if only my engineers could come up with something as efficient as that". The Italian thinks: "If only we could catch him, we could make lots of beautiful things with his hide". And the Finn thinks: "I wonder what the elephant thinks of me!".

❧ ❧

Eigenlijk zijn Finnen wat de deskundigen 'alles of niets drin-kers' noemen. Weken achtereen drinken ze geen druppel en dan ineens laten ze zich vollopen. De deskundigen zeggen ook, dat dit terug te voeren is op het niet eens zo verre verleden toen alle Finnen op het land werkten. Week in, week uit, zagen ze bijna geen mensen en hadden weinig gelegenheid om de teugels eens even te laten vieren. Als het dan marktdag was en ze verkocht hadden wat ze verbouwd hadden, wilden ze het geld ook wel eens laten rollen. Het daarom is het dan ook niet te verwonderen dat Finnen de indruk maken van een tamelijk introvert volk, zoals deze grap suggereert.

Drie zakenmensen, een Duitser, een Italiaan en een Fin, gaan op safari en plots komt er een reusachtige olifant te voorschijn uit de rimboe. De Duitser bekijkt het dier eens en denkt: "Wat een kracht heeft dat beest, stel je voor dat mijn ingenieurs zoiets grandioos konden bedenken". De Italiaan denkt: "Konden we het dier maar te pakken krijgen, er zijn van die huid allerlei prachtige dingen te maken". En de Fin denkt: "Ik vraag me af wat die olifant van me vindt ?"

En fait, les Finnois sont ce que les experts qualifient de "buveurs en société". Ils peuvent passer des semaines sans boire une goutte puis, brusquement, recourir à la dive bouteille. Selon les experts, à nouveau, cela remonte à l'époque - pas si ancienne - où tous les Finnois travaillaient la terre. Pendant des semaines, ils n'avaient que peu de contacts sociaux et pas d'occasion de décompresser - jusqu'au jour du marché où, ayant vendu leur production, ils avaient aussi un peu d'argent en poche. Pas étonnant que les Finnois donnent l'impression d'être introvertis, comme le laisse supposer cette blague.

Trois hommes d'affaires - un Allemand, un Italien et un Finnois - partent en safari. Un énorme éléphant s'avance nonchalamment hors de la jungle. L'Allemand regarde l'animal et pense : "Quelle bête puissante, si seulement mes ingénieurs pouvaient inventer quelque chose d'aussi efficace !". L'Italien pense : "Si seulement nous pouvions l'attraper, nous pourrions faire des tas de belles choses avec sa peau". Et le Finnois pense : "Je me demande ce que l'éléphant pense de moi !".

In Wirklichkeit sind die Finnen das, was die Fachleute als "Quartalssäufer" bezeichnen. Wochenlang trinken sie überhaupt nichts und plötzlich hängen sie dann an der Flasche. Die Experten erklären, das ginge alles auf die - nicht so lange zurückliegende - Zeit zurück, als alle Finnen noch in der Landwirtschaft beschäftigt waren. Menschliche Kontakte gab es nur wenig und kaum eine Gelegenheit, sich auszutoben, bis auf den Markttag, wenn sie ihre Ware verkauft und sogar etwas Geld übrig hatten. Kein Wunder, daß man die Finnen für introvertiert hält, wie aus diesem Witz hervorgeht.

Drei Geschäftsleute - ein Deutscher, ein Italiener und ein Finne - sind auf einer Safari und plötzlich spaziert ein riesiger Elefant aus dem Busch. Der Deutsche sieht sich das Tier an und denkt: "Was für ein mächtiges Biest, wenn meine Ingenieure doch nur sowas leistungsstarkes entwerfen könnten". Der Italiener denkt: "Wenn wir ihn doch nur erlegt hätten, was für viele schöne Dinge könnte man doch aus seiner Haut herstellen". Und der Finne denkt: "Was soll wohl der Elefant von mir denken !"

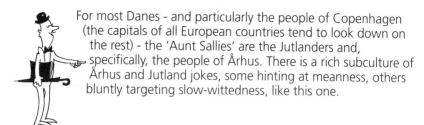

For most Danes - and particularly the people of Copenhagen (the capitals of all European countries tend to look down on the rest) - the 'Aunt Sallies' are the Jutlanders and, specifically, the people of Århus. There is a rich subculture of Århus and Jutland jokes, some hinting at meanness, others bluntly targeting slow-wittedness, like this one.

What does an Århuser do when he goes on the toilet?
He takes the door off so that nobody can peep through the keyhole.

❧ ☙

Voor de meeste Denen en vooral voor de mensen uit Kopenhagen (de inwoners van Europese hoofdsteden hebben allemaal de neiging neer te kijken op de mensen uit de rest van het land) zijn de Jutlanders en dan vooral de mensen uit Århus, het toppunt van domheid. Er doen heel wat grappen over Århus en de Jutlanders de ronde, die soms te maken hebben met gierigheid of keihard verwijzen naar het niet zo bij de pinken zijn, zoals deze.

Wat doet iemand uit Århus als hij naar de toilet gaat ?
Hij haalt de deur weg om zeker te zijn dat niemand door het sleutelgat kan kijken.

Les habitants du Jylland, et, plus précisément, ceux d'Århus, sont les souffre-douleur de la plupart des Danois, particulièrement ceux de Copenhague (les capitales de tous les pays européens ont tendance à snober le reste du pays). Il existe une riche sous-culture de blagues sur Århus et le Jylland : certaines suggèrent l'avarice; d'autres raillent sans ménagement la lenteur d'esprit, comme celle-ci.

Que fait un habitant d'Århus quand il va aux toilettes ?

Il enlève la porte pour que personne ne puisse regarder par le trou de la serrure.

Für die meisten Dänen und ganz besonders für die Leute aus Kopenhagen (alle Hauptstädte sämtlicher Länder in Europa neigen dazu, die anderen zu verachten), sind die Jütländer, vor allem die Einwohner von Århus richtige "Schießbudenfiguren". Es gibt eine reiche Subkultur an Witzen über Århus und Jütland. Einige dieser Witze weisen auf Knauserigkeit und andere, wie dieser, aus ausgesprochene Begriffsstutzigkeit hin.

Was tut ein Einwohner aus Århus, der zur Toilette muß ?

Er hängt die Tür aus, damit niemand durch das Schlüsselloch schauen kann.

There must be many 'smallest books' jokes around the globe. The European version is, like its subject, short and to the point. Where this joke originated is anybody's guess. It could be British, it could be American. Whatever, it is inaccurate. For a start, Italians are capable of great heroism, of a dashing and personal kind: they simply don't see the point in being used as cannon fodder, unlike many other Europeans. Norway considers it has eminent citizens as well as also-rans and the Dutch think their cooking is great (most of it is Indonesian). As for the Germans, they **do** have a sense of humour.

The smallest books in the world?
An Italian history of war heroes,
an anthology of German humour,
'Dutch Haute Cuisine'
and the Norwegian 'Who's Who?'.

❧ ❧

Grappen over het allerkleinste boekje vind je over de hele wereld. De Europese versie is kort maar krachtig. De herkomst van deze grap is in nevelen gehuld. Brits misschien of anders Amerikaans...hoe het ook zij, de grap berust op een misverstand, want Italianen kunnen best zeer heldhaftig zijn, maar op hun gans eigen flitsende manier. Ze zien er, in tegenstelling tot veel andere Europeanen, alleen het nut niet van in om zich als kanonnevoer te laten gebruiken. Noren hebben heel wat eminente figuren voortgebracht, maar lopen daar alleen niet zo mee te koop. Hollanders vinden dat ze uitstekend kunnen koken en Duitsers hebben weldegelijk gevoel voor humor.

Wat is het allerkleinste boekje ter wereld ?
Een historisch overzicht van Italiaanse oorlogshelden,
een bloemlezing van Duitse humor,
een Hollandse 'Haute Cuisine' kookboek
en de Noorse 'Who's Who?'.

Il doit circuler beaucoup d'histoires du "plus petit livre..." sur le globe. La version européenne, comme la matière du livre, est brève et percutante. Tout le monde se demande d'où provient cette blague. Elle pourrait être britannique, ou alors américaine. Quoi qu'il en soit, elle est inexacte. Premièrement, les Italiens sont capables d'un grand héroïsme, d'une nature personnelle et éclatante, mais ils ne voient tout simplement pas l'intérêt de servir de chair à canon, contrairement à de nombreux autres Européens. Les Norvégiens pensent que, parmi les quidams, ils comptent aussi d'éminents citoyens, et les Néerlandais estiment que leur cuisine est délicieuse (elle est le plus souvent d'inspiration indonésienne). Quant aux Allemands, ils ont de l'humour.

Les plus petits livres du monde ?
Une histoire italienne des héros de guerre,
une anthologie de l'humour allemand,
"Gastronomie néerlandaise"
et le "Who's Who?" norvégien.

❧ ❦

Über das "kleinste Buch" gibt es zahlreiche Witze in der ganzen Welt. Die europäische Fassung ist, genau wie der Gegenstand selbst, sehr kurz und treffend. Keiner weiß, woher dieser Witz eigentlich stammt, aus Amerika oder aus England. Auf jeden Fall ist die Pointe unzutreffend. Um es gleich zu sagen, die Italiener sind sehr wohl dazu imstande, große, verwegene und persönliche Heldentaten zu vollbringen: sie sehen bloß nicht ein, warum sie sich als Kanonenfutter verheizen lassen sollen, wie so viele andere Europäer. Die Norweger wissen, daß sie bedeutende Mitbürger aber auch solche in der Kategorie "ferner liefen" haben und die Holländer sind überzeugt, daß ihre (zumeist indonesische) Küche hervorragend ist. Und was die Deutschen betrifft, auch sie haben Sinn für Humor.

Das kleinste Buch der Welt ?
Eine Geschichte der italienische Kriegshelden,
eine Abhandlung über deutschen Humor,
ein Werk über holländische "Haute Cuisine"
und der norwegische "Who's Who ?".

The Dutch, a naturally and sensibly frugal people - except when they behave contrary to type, as more and more of them are doing these days - are the butt of a lot of 'mean' jokes.

Most such jokes, like the ones the Dutch tell about the Belgians, are pretty unsubtle. Here's one I happen to like. It purports to be a letter to the editor of a Dutch newspaper.

"Dear Sir,

If you persist in publishing silly jokes about the meanness of the Dutch, I will feel obliged to stop borrowing your newspaper from my neighbour."

De Nederlanders, van nature en terecht een zeer zuinig ingesteld volk, behalve wanneer ze daar tegen ingaan en dat komt de laatste tijd steeds meer voor, vormen het mikpunt van een heel reeks 'minne' grappen.

De meeste van dat soort grappen, zoals de Belgenmoppen, zijn alles behalve subtiel. Toch ben ik er een gekomen die ik goed vond. Het is zogenaamd een brief aan de redactie van een Nederlandse krant.

"Mijne Heren,

Als u in uw krant flauwe grappen blijft afdrukken over de gierigheid van de Nederlanders, zal ik mij genoodzaakt zien uw krant niet langer te lenen van mijn buurman."

Les Néerlandais, peuple naturellement économe, à bon escient - sauf lorsqu'ils font mentir le stéréotype, comme ils sont de plus en plus nombreux à le faire de nos jours - sont la cible de beaucoup de blagues sur l'avarice.

La plupart de ces blagues, tout comme celles que les Néerlandais racontent sur les Belges, manque légèrement de subtilité. En voici une que j'aime bien. Il est censé s'agir d'une lettre à l'éditeur d'un journal néerlandais.

"Monsieur,

Si vous continuez à publier de stupides plaisanteries sur l'avarice des Néerlandais, je me verrai contraint de cesser d'emprunter votre journal à mon voisin."

❧ ☙

Die Holländer sind von Natur aus ein vernünftigerweise sparsames Volk, ausgenommen dann, wenn sie aus der Art fallen, was immer häufiger vorzukommen scheint, und dann werden sie zur Zielscheibe einer Unzahl "bösartiger" Witze.

Die meisten dieser Witze sind, wie die von Holländern über Belgier erzählte, ziemlich albern. Aber hier ist einer, denn ich eigentlich mag. Es soll ein Schreiben an den Herausgeber einer holländischen Zeitung gewesen sein.

"Sehr geehrter Herr,

Wenn Sie weiterhin dumme Witze über die Knauserigkeit der Holländer veröffentlichen, sehe ich mich gezwungen, mir Ihre Zeitung nicht mehr von meinem Nachbarn auszuborgen."

The Dutch also have a reputation for being astute business folk, sometimes not entirely to their credit. This joke purports to find its origins in Germany, maybe in anticipation of (and retribution for) the 'mussels' joke that comes later in this book.

The Swiss federal transport authorities invite offers for the construction of a road tunnel under the Alps. To their surprise, the most competitive price comes from a Dutch partnership, Smeets & Kuypers. Uncertain of the competence of a Dutch company in drilling tunnels through solid rock, they summon Mr Smeets to justify his proposal. "It's like this", Smeets explains. "Kuypers and his team will start from the south side and I and my team will drill from the north. There's nothing to it: we just meet in the middle." "And if you don't?", query the Swiss. "Then you get two tunnels for the price of one."

❧ ❦

Van de Nederlanders wordt ook gezegd dat ze zakelijk van wanten weten en dat is lang niet altijd positief bedoeld. Naar verluidt zou deze grap uit Duitsland afkomstig zijn, misschien als voorloper of als reactie op de 'mossel' grappen verderop in dit boek.

De Zwitserse federale overheid voor het transportwezen heeft een aanbesteding uitgeschreven voor de bouw van een autotunnel door de Alpen. Wat schetst hun verbazing wanneer blijkt dat het beste bod is uitgebracht door twee Nederlandse partners, Smeets & Kuypers. Omdat men er enigszins aan twijfelt of een Nederlands bedrijf in staat is een tunnel door de rotsen te boren, verzoeken zij de heer Smeets nadere uitleg over het voorstel te geven: "Dat zit zo", legt Smeets uit. "Kuypers en zijn mensen beginnen aan de zuidkant en ik begin met mijn mensen aan de noordkant. En in het midden komen we bij elkaar, zo simpel is dat." "En als dat niet lukt", vragen de Zwitsers. "Dan krijgt u twee tunnels voor de prijs van één."

Les Néerlandais ont également la réputation d'être des gens d'affaires avisés, ce qui, quelquefois, n'est pas entièrement à leur honneur. Cette blague nous viendrait d'Allemagne, et pourrait être l'offensive (ou la contre-attaque) correspondant à la "blague des moules", citée plus loin.

Les autorités fédérales suisses publient un appel d'offres pour la construction d'un tunnel routier sous les Alpes. A leur grande surprise, c'est une association néerlandaise, Smeets & Kuypers, qui cite le prix le plus compétitif. Doutant de la capacité d'une société néerlandaise à creuser des tunnels dans la roche dure, elles convoquent M. Smeets pour qu'il étaie sa proposition. "Voilà", explique Smeets. "Kuypers et son équipe partiront du sud, moi et mon équipe du nord. Inévitablement, nous allons nous rencontrer au milieu." "Et si ce n'est pas le cas ?" questionne le Suisse. "Alors, vous aurez deux tunnels pour le prix d'un."

❧ ❦

Die Holländer stehen auch im Ruf, ganz besonders gewiefte Geschäftsleute zu sein, was nicht immer gut gemeint ist. Dieser Witz soll in Deutschland entstanden sein, möglicherweise im Vorgriff auf (und als Rache für) die "Muschel"-Witze, mit denen wir uns weiter im Text befassen werden.

Die Schweizerischen Verkehrsbehörden ersuchen um Angebote für den Bau eines Straßentunnels unter den Alpen. Zu ihrer Überraschung kommt das günstigste Angebot von der holländischen Firma Smeets & Kuypers. Da sie doch ihre Zweifel bezüglich des fachlichen Könnens eines holländischen Unternehmens beim Bohren von Tunnels durch harte Felsen hegen, verlangen sie von Herrn Smeets, sein Angebot zu rechtfertigen. "Das ist so", erklärt Herr Smeets, "Kuypers und sein Team beginnt an der Südseite und ich bohre mit meinem Team an der Nordseite. Überhaupt kein Problem: wir treffen uns einfach in der Mitte." "Und falls nicht ?", gibt der Schweizer zu bedenken. "Dann kriegen Sie einfach zwei zum Preis von einem Tunnel."

This one may have Afrikaans origins (it is quoted in James Mitchener's book, *"The Covenant"*, though not quite in this form). No doubt the Dutch would use it on the Belgians, the Belgians on the Dutch, the Swedes on the Norwegians, the Norwegians on the Swedes, and so on...

Henk is putting up a flagpole. He makes a hole in the ground, puts the pole in, then climbs up with a tape to measure it. The flagpole falls over. Herman, who is watching him, says: "Look, Henk, why don't you measure the flagpole while it's still on the ground?". "Don't be silly", says Henk, "I want to measure the height, not the length".

❦ ❦

Wie weet is deze grap van Afrikaanse herkomst (het verhaal staat in een iets andere versie in het boek van James Mitchener: *"The Convenant"*). Maar de Hollanders vertellen vast hetzelfde verhaal over de Belgen en omgekeerd, de Zweden over de Noren en omgekeerd en ga zo maar door...

Henk wil een vlaggestok in de grond zetten. Eerst maakt hij een gat en zet de stok recht, klimt er dan om te meten. De vlaggestok valt om. Dan zegt Herman, die staat toe te kijken: "Zeg, Henk, kan je die stok niet beter meten terwijl die nog op de grond ligt ?". Henk antwoordt daarop: "Doe niet zo onnozel, ik wil toch de hoogte meten, niet de lengte".

Celle-ci pourrait être d'origine afrikaner (elle est citée sous une forme quelque peu différente dans l'ouvrage de James Mitchener "The Covenant"). Il ne fait pas de doute que les Néerlandais la raconteraient sur les Belges, les Belges sur les Néerlandais, les Suédois sur les Norvégiens, les Norvégiens sur les Suédois et ainsi de suite...

Henk dresse un mât. Il creuse un trou dans le sol, y plante le mât, puis grimpe sur le mât avec un mètre-ruban pour le mesurer. Le mât culbute. Herman, qui le regarde, lui dit: "Ecoute, Henk, pourquoi tu ne mesures pas le mât pendant qu'il est encore par terre ?" "Ne sois pas idiot", réplique Henk. "Je veux mesurer sa hauteur, pas sa longueur."

❧ ❦

Ursprünglich könnte dies sehr wohl ein Afrikaaner-Witz gewesen sein (er wird im Buch von James Mitchener "The Covenant" erzählt, wenn auch nicht in der absolut gleichen Form). Zweifellos würden die Holländer ihn über die Belgier, die Belgier über die Holländer, die Schweden über die Norweger, die Norweger über die Schweden, usw., erzählen.

Henk richtet einen Fahnenmast auf. Er gräbt zuerst ein Loch in den Boden, stellt den Mast hinein, dann klettert er mit einem Meterband zum Messen hinauf. Der Fahnenmast fällt um. Hermann, der ihm zuschaut, sagt darauf hin :" Sieh' mal her, Henk, warum hast Du den Mast nicht gemessen, solange er flach auf der Erde lag ?" "Sei doch nicht blöd, Mann", sagt Henk, "Ich will doch die Höhe und nicht die Länge messen".

Lots of jokes are told about the Belgians by their neighbours - the Dutch, the French and, to a lesser extent, the Germans who generally can't be bothered. Most of these jokes are stupid and say more about the perpetrators than their victims. The best Belgian jokes are the ones they tell about one another ('one another' being the Flemish and the Walloons, since the German-speaking Belgians can't be bothered either).

When we're in trouble, we talk. When the Walloons talk, they're in trouble. **(Flemish joke)**

A Flemish farmer set off in his Mercedes-Benz for Calais in northern France. When he got across the frontier he saw a signpost saying 'Pas de Calais'. So he turned round and went back home. **(Walloon joke)**

❧ ❧

Belgen zijn vaak het onderwerp van grappen verteld door hun buren, de Nederlanders, de Fransen en in mindere mate de Duitsers, die het doorgaans niet de moeite vinden. Deze grappen getuigen meestal van verregaande domheid en onthullen meer over de bedenkers dan over het mikpunt van de grappen. De beste Belgische grappen vertellen de Belgen over elkaar (met elkaar bedoelen ze dan de Vlamingen en de Walen, want ook hier komen de Duitssprekende Belgen in het verhaal niet voor).

Wanneer wij problemen hebben, gaan we praten. Als de Walen gaan praten, hebben ze problemen. **(Vlaamse grap)**

Een Vlaamse boer reed in zijn Mercedes naar Calais in Noord-Frankrijk. Bij de grens zag hij een bord met 'Pas de Calais'. Dus keerde hij om en ging weer naar huis. **(Waalse grap)**

Les Belges font l'objet de nombreuses blagues de la part de leurs voisins, les Néerlandais, les Français et, dans une moindre mesure, les Allemands, qui n'en prennent généralement pas la peine. La plupart de ces histoires sont stupides et en disent plus long sur les auteurs que sur les victimes. Les meilleures blagues belges sont celles qu'ils racontent les uns sur les autres ("les uns" et "les autres" étant les Flamands et les Wallons, car les Belges de langue allemande n'en prennent pas la peine non plus).

Lorsque nous avons des problèmes, nous parlons. Lorsque les Wallons parlent, ils ont des problèmes. **(blague flamande)**

Au volant de sa Mercedes, un fermier flamand part pour Calais, dans le nord de la France. Lorsqu'il passe la frontière, il voit une pancarte indiquant "Pas de Calais". Il fait demi-tour et rentre chez lui.

(blague wallonne)

❧ ❧

Über die Belgier erzählen die Nachbarn viele Witze, sowohl die Holländer als auch die Franzosen — Deutsche haben scheinbar dazu keine Lust. Die meisten dieser Witze sind blöde und sagen mehr über diejenigen aus, die sie verbrochen haben, als über die Zielscheibe ihres Gespötts. Am besten sind die belgische Witze, die sie voneinander erzählen ('voneinander' bezieht sich hier auf die Flamen und die Wallonen, denn auch die deutschsprachigen Belgier sind nur wenig interessiert).

Wenn wir Schwierigkeiten haben, dann reden wir. Wenn die Wallonen reden, dann bekommen sie Schwierigkeiten. **(flämischer Witz)**

Ein flämischer Landwirt fährt mit seinem Mercedes nach Calais in Nordfrankreich. In Frankreich angelangt, sieht er ein Schild mit 'Pas de Calais'. Darauf macht er kehrt und fährt enttäuscht wieder nach Hause.

(wallonischer Witz)

Jokes about Belgians and French fries ('chips' to the British) would fill a book on their own. They are justified, because Belgian frites are delicious, although more foreigners seem to eat them now than Belgians. The Dutch are no exception...

Where is the biggest chip stall in the world? On the frontier between Holland and France.

If you see a man dead in the street clutching a packet of frites/fritten (chips to the English, French fries to the Americans), then he's a Belgian. If you see a passer-by take the packet from the dead man's hand, he's a Dutchman...

Er bestaan zoveel grappen over Belgen en frieten, dat daar alleen al een boek mee te vullen valt. En met rede, want Belgische frieten zijn inderdaad heel erg lekker, hoewel het erop lijkt dat de buitenlanders ze tegenwoordig meer eer aandoen dan de Belgen zelf... Vooral de Nederlanders zijn grote liefhebbers.

Waar staat de grootste frietkot ter wereld ? Op de grens tussen Frankrijk en Nederland.

Als u iemand dood op straat ziet liggen met een zak friet in zijn hand, kan dat niet anders dan een Belg zijn. Als u iemand voorbij ziet komen die de Belg zijn zak friet afneemt, kunt u er zeker van zijn dat het een Hollander is.

A elles seules, les histoires de Belges et de frites suffiraient à remplir un livre. Elles sont justifiées, car les frites belges sont délicieuses, bien qu'à l'heure actuelle, les étrangers semblent en consommer plus que les Belges. Les Néerlandais ne font pas exception...

Où se trouve la plus grande friterie du monde ? Sur la frontière entre les Pays-Bas et la France.

Si tu vois en rue un homme mort, serrant dans sa main un cornet de frites, tu sais que c'est un Belge. Si tu vois un autre homme lui prendre le cornet de frites, tu sais que c'est un Néerlandais.

❦ ❦

Witze über Belgier und Fritten (von den Deutschen auch "Pommes" genannt) würden allein schon ein ganzes Buch füllen. Richtig ist das schon, denn belgische "Pommes frites" schmecken köstlich und schon heute verspeist man mehr davon im Ausland als in Belgien. Die Holländer zählen dabei kaum zu den Ausnahmen...

Wo gibt es den größten Frittenstand der Welt ? Zwischen der holländischen und der französischen Grenze !

Sieht man einen Toten, mit einer Frittentüte in der Hand, auf der Straße liegen, dann kann es nur ein Belgier sein. Wenn jemand ihm die Frittentüte aus der Hand nimmt, dann ist es bestimmt ein Holländer.

This one has to be the ultimate 'let's-be-nasty-to-our-neighbours' joke: it's a Dutch joke about the Belgians. It's also unusual in that it takes a passing swipe at a domestic scapegoat - in this case the Dutch Limburgers who, in the view of the rest of the Netherlands, are so un-Dutch as to be virtually Belgian. It's quite a clever joke and may need a moment's thought (there may also be a bit of wishful thinking here).

Q: What would happen to the average IQ of the Netherlands and Belgium if the Dutch province of Limburg was transferred to Belgium?

A: The average IQ of both the Netherlands and Belgium would go up.

＊ ＊

Deze grap is zo ongeveer het summum in de categorie 'van je buren moet je het maar hebben'. Het is een Nederlandse grap over de Belgen. Tussendoor krijgt een zondebok voor binnenlands gebruik er ook nog even van langs. In dit geval zijn dat de Nederlandse Limburgers, die volgens hun landgenoten in niets op de Nederlanders lijken en dus eigenlijk nagenoeg Belgen zijn. Een intelligente grap, een doordenkertje dus en wie weet is de wens ook wel de vader van de gedachte.

Vraag: Hoe zou het staan met het gemiddelde IQ van de Nederlanders en de Belgen, als Nederlands Limburg bij België kwam te horen ?

Antwoord: Het gemiddelde IQ van de Nederlanders en de Belgen zou omhoog gaan.

Celle-ci est sans doute la plus vilaine des blagues de la catégorie "soyons-méchants-avec-nos-voisins" : c'est une blague néerlandaise sur les Belges. Elle est également originale, en ce sens qu'elle égratigne au passage des têtes de Turc locales (ici, les Néerlandais du Limbourg qui, aux yeux du reste des Pays-Bas, sont tellement peu néerlandais qu'ils sont pour ainsi dire belges). C'est une blague assez fine qui requerra peut-être un moment de réflexion (on pourrait aussi y déceler l'ombre d'un souhait).

Q : *Comment le Quotient Intellectuel de la population néerlandaise et belge se comporterait-il si la province néerlandaise du Limbourg était transférée en Belgique ?*

R. : *Le QI augmenterait autant aux Pays-Bas qu'en Belgique.*

☙ ❧

Dies müßte eigentlich das Nonplusultra eines Witzes sein, mit dem man "scheußlich" zu Nachbarn sein will: die Holländer erzählen ihn über die Belgier. Ungewöhnlich ist er auch, weil er so nebenbei einem inländischen Sündenbock eins auswischt, in diesem Falle den holländischen Limburgern, die nach Ansicht der übrigen Holländer so unholländisch sind, daß man sie fast als Belgier bezeichnen könnte. Der Witz ist ziemlich clever und könnte einiger Überlegung bedürfen (möglicherweise steckt auch ein gewisses Wunschdenken dahinter).

Frage: *Was würde wohl mit der durchschnittlichen Intelligenzquote in den Niederlanden und in Belgien geschehen, wenn die holländische Provinz Limburg bei Belgien angeschlossen würde?*

Antwort: *Die Durchschnittsquote würde sowohl in den Niederlanden als auch in Belgien steigen.*

Despite reports to the contrary, the average Belgian is a kind-hearted soul addicted to adopting stray animals. The following joke, which was no doubt invented by the French or the Dutch with the intention of showing how stupid the Belgians are, may inadvertently support this view. The joke is set in a town in northern France.

A Belgian found a monkey and asked a gendarme what he should do with it. The gendarme told him to take the animal to the zoo. The next day the gendarme saw the man walking along holding hands with the monkey. "Look", said the gendarme, "I thought I told you to take the monkey to the zoo". "Yes", said the Belgian, "We went to the zoo yesterday. Today we're going to the cinema".

❧ ❦

Hoewel het tegendeel vaak beweerd wordt, is de gemiddelde Belg een goedmenende ziel die het niet kan laten om dieren zonder baas te adopteren. Deze grap werd vast en zeker bedacht door een Fransman of een Hollander die daarmee wilde aantonen hoe dom de Belgen zijn, maar lijkt eerder ongewild een illustratie te zijn van het eerste standpunt.

Het verhaal speelt zich af ergens in Noord-Frankrijk.

Een Belg heeft een aap gevonden en vraagt aan een gendarme wat hij ermee moet doen. Hij zegt hem de aap naar de dierentuin te brengen. De volgende dag komt de gendarme de man tegen, hand in hand met de aap. "Wat", zegt de gendarme, "ik had toch gezegd dat die aap naar de dierentuin moest". "Ja", zegt de Belg, "Gisteren zijn we naar de dierentuin geweest. En vandaag gaan we naar de film".

En dépit de rumeurs indiquant le contraire, le Belge moyen est une bonne âme qui ne peut s'empêcher d'adopter des animaux errants. La blague suivante, sans aucun doute inventée par les Français ou les Néerlandais dans le but de montrer à quel point les Belges sont stupides, pourrait, par inadvertance, conforter ce point de vue. L'histoire se déroule dans une ville du nord de la France.

Un Belge trouve un singe et demande à un gendarme ce qu'il doit en faire. Le gendarme lui dit d'emmener l'animal au zoo. Le lendemain, le gendarme voit l'homme se promener main dans la main avec le singe. "Dites", fait le gendarme, "il me semblait vous avoir dit d'emmener le singe au zoo". "Oui", dit le Belge, "nous sommes allés au zoo hier. Aujourd'hui, nous allons au cinéma."

Trotz entgegenlautender Gerüchte ist der Normalbelgier ein gutherziger Mensch, der herrenlose Tiere liebevoll adoptiert. Der folgende Witz dürfte wohl von Franzosen oder Holländern mit der Absicht erfunden worden sein, die Begriffsstutzigkeit der Belgier vorzuführen, aber ungewollt dürfte er wohl gerade diese Tierliebe unter Beweis stellen. Der Ort der Handlung ist eine Stadt in Nordfrankreich.

Ein Belgier findet einen streunenden Affen und fragt einen Gendarmen, was er damit tun sollte. Dieser rät ihm, das Tier zum Zoo zu bringen. Am nächsten Tag sieht der Gendarm den Belgier Hand in Hand mit dem Affen spazieren gehen. "Hören Sie mal", sagt der Gendarm, "Ich hatten Ihnen doch gesagt, den Affen zum Zoo zu bringen". "Ja sicher", antwortet der Belgier, "im Zoo waren wir gestern, heute gehen wir ins Kino".

This French joke about the Belgians is as patronising as any of the others, but it does have the benefit of being mildly ingenious (for an intrinsically intelligent people, it is extraordinary how silly the French can be when inventing these jokes).

A Belgian rents a villa on Spain's Costa Brava for the family's summer holidays. On arrival, before it gets dark, he rushes around the house putting up insect screens on all the windows with netting he has brought with him from Brussels: fine-mesh netting to stop the midges and larger-mesh netting to stop the mosquitos...

❦ ❧

Deze Franse Belgenmop getuigt net als alle andere van de gebruikelijke laatdunkendheid, maar deze gaat toch iets meer in de richting van een doordenkertje (het is opmerkelijk dat een verder toch intelligent volk als de Fransen zulke onnozele grappen kan bedenken).

Een Belg huurt een villa aan de Spaanse Costa Brava voor een zomervakantie voor het hele gezin. Na aankomst heeft hij het druk als een klein baasje. Overal moeten namelijk voor het donker, horren komen tegen de insekten. Het gaas heeft hij meegebracht uit Brussel: gaas met fijne mazen tegen de muggen en gaas met grotere mazen tegen de muskieten...

Dans cette blague, comme dans toutes les autres, les Français prennent les Belges de haut, mais celle-ci a pour elle une certaine inventivité (pour un peuple intrinsèquement intelligent, c'est incroyable à quel point les Français peuvent être stupides lorsqu'ils inventent ces blagues).

Pour les vacances d'été de sa famille, un Belge loue une villa sur la Costa Brava espagnole. A son arrivée, avant la tombée de la nuit, il contourne fébrilement la maison pour fixer devant chaque fenêtre des moustiquaires fabriquées avec du tulle amené de Bruxelles : du tulle à mailles fines pour arrêter les petits moustiques et du tulle à grosses mailles pour arrêter les gros...

※ ※

Dieser französische Witz über die Belgier ist herablassend wie die anderen auch, aber er hat den Vorteil, etwas raffinierter zu sein (für ein an sich intelligentes Volk ist es höchst erstaunlich, wie dümmlich die Franzosen beim Erfinden dieser Witze sein können).

Ein Belgier mietet für den Sommerurlaub seiner Familie eine Villa an der spanischen Costa Brava. Bei seiner Ankunft rennt er um das Haus, um vor der Dunkelheit noch rasch alle aus Belgien mitgebrachten Netzgewebe zum Schutz vor Insekten an den Fenstern anzubringen: feinmaschiges gegen Mücken und grobmaschiges gegen Moskitos...

Although the easygoing Belgians have no trouble with jokes told against them (though they seem to be more indulgent to French jokes than the Dutch variety), they do occasionally get stung into retaliation. In fact, most jokes told about the Belgians are so stupid they elicit little more than groans. The retaliation, on the other hand, is often shrewd and sharp, like this Belgian joke about the French.

What's the quickest way to make a profit?

Buy a Frenchman for what he's worth and sell him for what he thinks he's worth.

Belgen nemen doorgaans de grappen die er over ze gemaakt worden, gemoedelijk op. Hoewel ze minder moeite lijken te hebben met wat er uit Frankrijk komt dan wat de Hollanders bedenken. Van tijd tot tijd geven ze ook weerwerk. Meestal zijn Belgenmoppen van een domheid die alleen maar gekreun teweegbrengt. Maar de grappen waarmee de Belgen terugslaan zijn vaak scherp en pienter zoals deze over de Fransen.

Wat is de snelste manier om winst te maken ?

Een Fransman kopen voor wat hij waard is en hem verkopen voor wat hij denkt dat hij waard is.

Bien que les Belges, accommodants, ne soient pas importunés par les blagues que l'on raconte sur eux (même s'ils semblent être plus indulgents vis-à-vis des blagues françaises que vis-à-vis des néerlandaises), ils sont parfois piqués au point de répliquer. En fait, la plupart des blagues racontées sur les Belges sont tellement stupides qu'elles provoquent à peine un couinement. La riposte, par contre, est souvent fine et rapide, comme cette blague belge sur les Français.

Quelle est la plus rapide manière de s'enrichir ?

Achetez un Français pour ce qu'il vaut et revendez-le au prix qu'il s'estime.

⁂

Obwohl die gelassenen Belgier sich die gegen sie gerichteten Witze problemlos (nachsichtiger bei französischen als bei holländischen Witzen) anhören, lassen sie sich doch zuweilen dazu hinreißen, Vergeltung zu üben. In Wirklichkeit sind die meisten Witze über die Belgier so doof, daß sie kaum mehr als ein überdrüssiges Grunzen hervorrufen können. Die Vergeltung jedoch kann scharf und verschmitzt sein, so wie dieser belgische Witz über die Franzosen.

Wie kann man schnellstens viel Geld verdienen ?

Man kauft einfach einen Franzosen zum richtigen Wert und verkauft ihn dann zum Wert, den er zu haben glaubt.

This joke is supposed to have been told, many years ago, by the Poles about the Prussians (whatever happened to the Prussians? It seems they went the same way as the ancient Greeks).

It's an intelligent joke because it tells you something about German respect for order (Lenin is reputed to have said the Germans always buy platform tickets before they storm a railway station). It also hints that the Germans are not the most talkative people in the world, though I know some exceptions.

A German child, twelve years old, has never spoken a word in his life. Over dinner one evening he turns to his parents and says "Salz, bitte" ('salt, please'). His astonished parents ask him why, if he could speak, he had never said anything till now. His reply: "bis heute war alles in Ordnung" ('up to now everything was OK').

❧ ❦

Het verhaal wil dat de Polen lang geleden deze grap vertelden over de Pruisen (wat is er eigenlijk geworden van de Pruisen ? Het lijkt erop dat het ze net zo vergaan is als de oude Grieken).

Deze grap is intelligent omdat het een verhelderend licht werpt op het Duitse gevoel voor orde (aan Lenin komt de eer toe gezegd te hebben dat de Duitsers voor ze een station bestormen altijd eerst een perronkaartje kopen). Ook wordt er gesuggereerd dat Duitsers alles behalve spraakzaam zijn, maar mij is al vaak gebleken dat er uitzonderingen zijn.

Een Duits kind van twaalf, heeft nog nooit een woord gesproken. Op een avond richt hij zich aan tafel tot zijn ouders en zegt 'het zout, graag'. Zijn stomverbaasde ouders, vragen waarom hij, hoewel hij kon praten, al die tijd niets gezegd heeft. En hij antwoordt: 'tot nu toe was alles in orde'.

Cette blague aurait été racontée, il y a très longtemps de cela, par les Polonais sur les Prussiens (où donc ont disparu les Prussiens ? Il semble qu'ils aient pris le même chemin que les anciens Grecs).

C'est une histoire intelligente, parce qu'elle vous donne une idée du respect germanique pour l'ordre (Lénine aurait dit que les Allemands achètent toujours des tickets de quai avant de prendre une gare d'assaut). Elle indique également que les Allemands ne sont pas des plus bavards, bien que je connaisse quelques exceptions.

Un petit Allemand de douze ans n'a jamais dit le moindre mot de toute sa vie. Un soir, au souper, il se tourne vers ses parents et dit "le sel, s'il vous plaît". Ses parents abasourdis lui demandent pourquoi, s'il savait parler, il n'a pas dit un seul mot jusque là - à quoi il répond : "bis heute war alles in Ordnung" ("Jusqu'aujourd'hui, tout était en ordre").

❧ ❧

Diesen Witz sollen die Polen sich, vor vielen Jahren, über die Preußen erzählt haben (wo sind eigentlich die Preußen geblieben ? Scheinbar sind sie mit den alten Griechen in der Versenkung verschwunden).

Intelligent ist dieser Witz, weil er eine Aussage über den deutschen Respekt für die Ordnung enthält (Lenin soll gesagt haben, daß die Deutschen zuerst eine Bahnsteigkarte lösen, ehe sie den Bahnhof stürmen). Er deutet auch darauf hin, daß die Deutschen nicht sehr gesprächig sein sollen, obwohl mir dazu manche Ausnahmen einfallen könnten.

Ein deutsches, zwölf Jahre altes Kind hat noch nie in seinem Leben ein Wort gesagt. Beim Abendessen sagt es plötzlich zu seinen Eltern "Salz, bitte". Die erstaunten Eltern möchten jetzt wissen, warum der Junge bis dato stumm geblieben ist. Seine Antwort : "Bis heute war alles in Ordnung !"

There's a story about a country boy from Kansas on a visit to Paris who, when pressed to say a few words in French, retorts: "Say, if English was good enough for Jesus Christ, it's good enough for me!".

The British could offer the same alibi but, being superficially fair-minded and disinclined to invoke superior authority, they prefer to tackle the issue head-on. The joke came to us from Germany.

Sir Alec returns to his London club, fresh from his holiday in France. "Did you have a good time?", his friends ask him. "Yes, fantastic", he says. "Did you have any problems with the language?". "No", says Sir Alec, "I didn't, but the French did."

※ ❦

Kent u die grap van die boerekinkel uit Kansas die naar Parijs gaat... En als ze hem vragen iets in het Frans te zeggen, komt het antwoord: "Zeg, als Jesus het alleen met Engels afkon, doe ik het daar ook wel mee!".

Van de Britten zou men iets dergelijks kunnen verwachten, maar omdat ze iedereen een kans willen geven en zich niet superieur willen opstellen, hebben ze hun eigen manier op het taalprobleem uit de wereld te helpen. Zoals blijkt uit deze grap die ons verteld werd door een Duitser.

Sir Alec komt na vakantie in Frankrijk terug in zijn Londense club.

Zijn vrienden vragen: "prettige vakantie gehad ?" "Ja, schitterend", luidt het antwoord. "Geen problemen met de taal ?". "Nee", is het antwoord van Sir Alec, "Ik niet, maar de Fransen wel."

C'est l'histoire d'un campagnard du Kansas en visite à Paris, à qui l'on demande avec insistance de dire quelques mots en français. "Dis, si Jésus-Christ a trouvé que l'anglais était assez bon pour lui, je m'en satisferai aussi !"

Les Britanniques pourraient invoquer le même alibi. Etant donné qu'ils sont superficiellement impartiaux et répugnent d'en appeler à une autorité supérieure, ils préfèrent attaquer le sujet de front. L'histoire suivante nous est parvenue via l'Allemagne.

Après avoir été en vacances en France, Sir Alec revient à son club londonien. "C'était bien ?" lui demandent ses amis. "Fantastique," répond-il. "N'avez-vous pas eu de difficultés avec la langue ?" "Non," réplique Sir Alec. "Pas moi, mais les Français, par contre..."

❧ ❧

Es gibt da die Geschichte von den Bauern aus Kansas, der Paris besucht und auf die Bitte hin, etwas auf Französisch zu sagen, erwidert : "Wenn Englisch gut genug für Jesus Christus war, dann ist es gut genug für mich !"

Die Engländer könnten sich des gleichen Alibis bedienen, aber da sie etwas oberflächlich fair und nicht geneigt sind, sich auf eine höhere Autorität zu berufen, gehen sie solche Fragen direkt an. Den folgenden Witz haben wir in Deutschland gehört.

Sir Alec betritt seinen Londoner Club, nach einem Urlaub in Frankreich. "Hast Du Dich gut amüsiert ?" fragen seine Freunde. "Es war phantastisch", antwortet er begeistert. "Hast Du keine Probleme mit der Sprache gehabt ?". "Überhaupt nicht", sagt Sir Alec, "Probleme hatten nur die Franzosen."

Some people suggest the Germans don't have a sense of humour. They do, as the 'Sir Alec' joke indicates. The trouble is that a lot of German jokes invoke a type of humour which the rest of us find unfunny. We don't get the point. Often, though, there is a touch of irony, gentle or bitter. Here is an example of the gentler kind. It also happens to be a Frisian joke, as well as a joke about the Frisians...

A Frisian peasant woman is lying on her deathbed. Her husband and children are standing next to her, sobbing.

Despite her enfeebled state, the dying woman finds the strength to comfort her husband. "When I'm gone", she says, "if you can't cope with the children, marry the Widow Tebben. She would be a good woman for you!"

"Yes", sobs her husband, "I've already thought of that."

❧ ❧

Er wordt beweerd dat Duitsers geen gevoel voor humor hebben. De 'Sir Alec' grap toont aan dat dat wel zo is. Het vervelende is dat veel Duitse grappen een soort humor hanteren waar de rest van ons het leuke niet van inziet. We snappen niet wat er grappig aan is. Vaak gaat het om goedaardige of bijtende ironie. Dit is er een van de goedaardige soort. Daar komt nog bij dat het een Friese grap is die ook nog over de Friezen gaat...

Een Friese boerin ligt op haar sterfbed en haar man en kinderen staan er snikkend omheen.

Ze is al zeer zwak, toch heeft de stervende vrouw nog de kracht om haar echtgenoot te troosten. "Als ik er niet meer ben", zegt ze, "en je redt het niet met de kinderen, trouw dan met de Weduwe Tebben. Dat zou een goede vrouw voor je zijn!"

"Ja", zegt de snikkende man, "daar had ik ook al aan gedacht."

Certaines personnes prétendent que les Allemands n'ont pas de sens de l'humour. C'est faux, comme le prouve la "blague de Sir Alec". Le problème, c'est que beaucoup de blagues allemandes font appel à un type d'humour que le reste d'entre nous ne trouve pas drôle. Nous restons perplexes. Souvent, pourtant, il y a une touche d'ironie, légère ou amère. Voici un exemple d'ironie légère. Il se fait que c'est une blague frisonne, tout autant qu'une blague sur les Frisons...

Une paysanne frisonne est couchée sur son lit de mort. Son mari et ses enfants sont debout à côté d'elle, en pleurs.

Malgré son état affaibli, la mourante trouve la force de réconforter son mari. "Quand je ne serai plus", dit-elle, "si tu ne t'en sors pas avec les enfants, épouse la Veuve Tebben. Elle ferait une bonne femme pour toi !"

"Oui", sanglote son mari, "j'y ai déjà pensé."

❦ ❦

Manche Menschen deuten an, die Deutschen hätten keinen Sinn für Humor. Das stimmt aber nicht, wie das Beispiel von "Sir Alec" beweist. Das Problem liegt darin, daß vielen deutschen Witzen eine Art von Humor zugrundeliegt, die die anderen gar nicht komisch finden. Häufig enthalten sie jedoch ein Quentchen leiser oder bitterer Ironie. Hier ist ein Beispiel der leisen Art. Zufällig ist es auch ein friesischer Witz und zugleich ein Witz über die Friesen...

Eine friesische Bauersfrau liegt auf dem Sterbebett. Ihr Mann und die Kinder stehen schluchzend um sie herum.

Mit schwacher Stimme bemüht die Sterbende sich, ihren Mann zu trösten. "Wenn ich nicht mehr bin", sagt sie, "und wenn Du mit den Kindern nicht zurecht kommst, dann heirate die Witwe Tebben. Sie wäre Dir ein gutes Weib !".

"Ja sicher", schluchzt der Mann, "daran hab ich auch bereits gedacht."

Germans are renowned and envied for their Wanderlust (envied because they have more money than the others to indulge it). They turn up in the most exotic places: Hawaii, Thailand, the North Sea island of Sylt, even Sicily.

Despite allegations to the contrary, they can even tell jokes against themselves, something that the French have difficulty in doing. Here's one of those jokes.

A group of German tourists makes its way to the top of Mount Etna and looks into the reeking and smokefilled crater. One of them turns to his neighbour and says, "it looks just like hell". The Italian guide hears this, shakes his head and mutters: "Oh, these Germans, they've been everywhere!"

❦ ❦

De Duitsers zijn beroemd om hun *Wanderlust* (en ook benijd omdat ze meer geld hebben om overal heen te trekken). In de verste uithoeken van de wereld komt men ze tegen: Hawaï, Thailand, Sylt, dat eiland in de Noordzee en zelfs op Sicilië.

En wat boze tongen ook mogen bewegen, ze kunnen weldegelijk de draak met zichzelf steken. Iets waartoe de Fransen absoluut niet in staat zijn. Een voorbeeld:

Een groep Duitse toeristen beklimt de Etna, ze bereiken de top en kijken in de onwelriekende, dampende krater. Zegt de ene Duitser tegen de andere: "lijkt veel op de hel". De Italiaanse gids, die dit hoort, mompelt hoofdschuddend: "die Duitsers, ze komen toch ook overal !"

Les Allemands sont réputés (et enviés) pour leur Wanderlust (amour du voyage). Enviés, parce qu'ils ont plus d'argent que les autres pour s'y consacrer. On les retrouve dans les endroits les plus exotiques : Hawaii, la Thaïlande, l'île de Sylt, en Mer du Nord, et même la Sicile.

Malgré tout ce qu'on a pu prétendre, ils peuvent même raconter des histoires sur eux-mêmes, ce que les Français ont peine à faire. En voici une.

Un groupe de touristes allemands arrive au sommet de l'Etna et plonge le regard dans le cratère fumant et nauséabond. L'un d'eux se tourne vers son voisin et dit : "On dirait tout à fait l'enfer". Le guide italien l'entend, secoue la tête et marmonne : "Ah, ces Allemands, ils ont vraiment été partout !"

Die Deutschen sind bekannt und beneidet für ihre Wanderlust (der Neid kommt auch wohl daher, daß sie mehr Geld zum Reisen haben). Überall tauchen sie auf, an den meistexotischen Flecken der Erde : Hawaii, Thailand, auf der Nordseeinsel Sylt, sogar auf Sizilien.

Trotz entgegenlautender Behauptungen, haben sie auch Sinn für Humor. Sie können sogar Witze über sich selbst reißen, was die Franzosen nur schwer zustande bringen. Es folgt ein solcher Witz.

Ein Gruppe deutsche Touristen besteigt den Ätna und schaut in den übelriechenden und raucherfüllten Krater. Ein Tourist sagt zum anderen : "So sieht's in der Hölle aus". Das hört der italienische Reisebegleiter, er schüttelt den Kopf und murmelt : "Diese Deutschen, überall sind sie schon gewesen !"

Further evidence both of this Wanderlust and of the Germans' capacity for laughing at themselves is provided by this true story told to me by the BA pilot concerned. The reference in the punchline reflects a Teutonic holiday habit which has now entered into European folklore. The Germans are, after all, renowned for their territoriality.

A British Airways 747 is lined up on the runway approach at Frankfurt airport, ready for take-off, when a Lufthansa jumbo rolls up in front. The pilot remonstrates with his opposite number over the radio. "Sorry, friend", says the Lufthansa pilot, "we got our towel on the runway first!".

Nog een bewijs van deze *Wanderlust* en de zelfspot waartoe de Duitsers in staat zijn, levert dit waar gebeurde verhaal dat mij verteld werd door de Britse piloot die het zelf had meegemaakt. Hierin wordt verwezen naar een vakantiegewoonte van de Germanen die deel is gaan uitmaken van de Europese folklore. Want de Duitsers staan immers bekend om hun territoriumdrift.

Een Britse 747 staat in de rij op de startbaan, klaar om op te stijgen uit Frankfurt. Ineens taxiët er een jumbo van de Lufthansa voorbij die voordringt. De Britse piloot geeft via de boordradio blijk van zijn ongenoegen. "Spijtig, beste vriend", zegt de Lufthansa-piloot, "maar onze handdoek lag hier eerst".

L'histoire vraie que m'a racontée ce pilote de la BA constitue une autre démonstration de cette Wanderlust et de la faculté des Allemands à rire d'eux-mêmes. La chute fait allusion à une habitude des Teutons en vacances, aujourd'hui entrée dans les traditions européennes. Les Allemands, après tout, sont connus pour leur sens du territoire.

Un 747 de la British Airways se trouve en bout de la piste d'envol à l'aéroport de Francfort, prêt à décoller, lorsqu'un jumbo-jet de la Lufthansa passe devant. Par la radio, le pilote fait des remontrances à son homologue. "Désolé, l'ami", dit le pilote de la Lufthansa, "nous étions les premiers à pendre notre serviette sur la piste!"

❦ ❦

Ein weiteres Beispiel für diese Wanderlust und die deutsche Fähigkeit, über sich selbst zu lachen, geht aus dieser wahren Geschichte hervor, die mir der betroffene der britischen BA-Fluggesellschaft selbst erzählt hat. Die Bemerkung in der Pointe weist auf eine teutonische Urlaubssitte hin, die bereits in die europäische Folklore eingegangen ist. Die Deutschen sind ja schließlich für ihre Revieransprüche bekannt.

"Eine 747 der British Airways steht abflugbereit auf der Startbahn des Frankfurter Flughafens als plötzlich ein Jumbo der Lufthansa sich vordrängt. Der BA-Pilot macht seinem Kollegen in der andern Maschine Vorhaltungen über den Funk. "Tut mir leid, mein Freund", sagt der Lufthansa-Pilot, "aber wir hatten die Startbahn schon mit dem Badetuch reserviert!".

I fondly thought of this as a German joke until I came across a book of Czech humour, where the role of the two Bavarians was taken by a pair of Czech militiamen. Probably the same joke is told by the French about the Bretons and the Greeks about the Pontic Greeks. Anyway, I like it.

Two Bavarians are standing on a Munich street corner when a Berliner comes up to them and asks the way to the Frauenkirche. They pretend not to understand his German so, calling their bluff, he addresses them in English, then French, then Italian. Eventually he walks off. "Impressive", says the first Bavarian, "all those languages". "So what", replies his friend, "it got him nowhere".

❧ ❧

Ik dacht eerst dat dit een Duitse grap was tot ik een boek met Tjechische humor in handen kreeg. Hierin waren de twee mannen uit Beieren vervangen door een stel Tjechische rijkswachters. Vermoedelijk bestaat er ook een Franse versie van met Bretoenen en vertellen de Grieken deze grap over de Pontische Grieken. Ik vind het in ieder geval een leuke grap.

Op de hoek van een straat in München staan twee Beierse mannen en er komt een man uit Berlijn naar ze toe die de weg naar de Frauenkirche vraagt. Ze doen net alsof ze zijn Duits niet verstaan en de ander die ze een hak wil zetten, begint met Engels, dan Frans en dan Italiaans. Tenslotte gaat hij maar weg. "Toch wel indrukwekkend", zegt de eerste man, "al die talen die die man spreekt". "Nou en", antwoordt zijn vriend, "hij komt er nergens mee".

Je chérissais celle-ci, que je considérais comme une blague allemande, jusqu'à ce que je tombe sur un livre d'humour tchèque, où une paire de miliciens tchèques tient le rôle des deux Bavarois. Les Français racontent sûrement la même blague à propos des Bretons, et les Grecs à propos des Grecs pontiques. Quoi qu'il en soit, elle me plaît.

A Munich, deux Bavarois sont plantés au coin d'une rue. Un Berlinois s'avance vers eux et leur demande le chemin de la Frauenkirche.
Ils prétendent ne pas comprendre son allemand, de sorte que, relevant le défi, il leur adresse la parole en anglais, puis en français, puis en italien. Finalement, il s'en va. "Toutes ces langues, étonnant", dit le premier Bavarois". "Et alors", répond son ami, "à quoi bon ?".

❦ ❧

Ich dachte immer allzu kühn, dies wäre ein deutscher Witz, bis ich ein Buch mit tschechischem Humor entdeckte, in dem tschechischen Milizsoldaten die Rolle der beiden Bayern zugeteilt war. Wahrscheinlich erzählen die Franzosen den gleichen Witz über die Savoyarden und die Griechen über die pontischen Griechen. Auf jeden Fall gefällt er mir.

Zwei Bayern stehen an einer Münchener Straßenecke und ein vorbeigehender Berliner erkundigt sich nach dem Weg zur Frauenkirche. Sie tun als ob sie sein Deutsch nicht verstünden und um sie auf die Probe zu stellen, spricht er die beiden Bayern zuerst auf Englisch, dann auf Französisch und Italienisch an. Schließlich entfernt er sich. "Beeindruckend", sagt der erste Bayer, "diese vielen Sprachen". "Na und", antwortet sein Freund," weit ist er ja nicht damit gekommen."

I had to pluck up courage to include this joke in the book. Like most of the jokes the Dutch tell about their neighbours, German or Belgian, it's pretty blunt. It's also pretty black, yet a lot of people find it funny. The first time I told it in public, I was with a group of American MBAs chaperoned by a Belgian university professor. The Americans, in the interests of Political Correctness, were not at all sure whether to laugh. But the Belgian professor, for whom mussels are in any case a source of great enjoyment, nearly fell off his chair in appreciation. He saved the day.

How do Germans eat mussels?
They bang on the table and shout "aufmachen!".

❧ ❧

Ik heb mezelf moeten vermannen om deze grap op te nemen in het boek. Zoals de meeste grappen die Hollanders vertellen over hun buren, de Duitsers of de Belgen, is het een nogal botte grap. En ook nogal zwartgallig, maar de meeste mensen vinden het toch een goede grap. Het eerste publiek waarop ik deze grap losliet, was een groep Amerikaanse MBA's die begeleid werden door een Belgische professor. De Amerikanen, die toch al zo bezig zijn met wat politiek wel en niet correct is, wisten niet of dit om te lachen was. Maar de Belgische professor, die iemand was die toch al veel plezier beleefde aan mosselen, viel bijna van zijn stoel van het lachen. En daarmee was ik gered.

Hoe plegen de Duitsers mosselen te eten ?
Ze kloppen op tafel en roepen "aufmachen !"

J'ai dû rassembler tout mon courage pour reprendre cette blague dans mon livre. Comme la plupart des blagues que les Néerlandais racontent sur leurs voisins, Allemands ou Belges, elle est assez directe. Elle est aussi assez noire, mais beaucoup de gens la trouvent drôle. La première fois que je l'ai racontée en public, j'étais avec un groupe de MBA's américains chaperonnés par un professeur d'université belge. Les Américains, soucieux d'être "politiquement corrects", ne savaient pas très bien s'ils devaient rire. Mais le professeur belge, pour qui, en tout cas, les moules sont une source de réel plaisir, est venu à mon secours, tombant presque de sa chaise en signe de contentement.

Comment les Allemands mangent-ils leurs moules ?
Ils tambourinent sur la table et crient : "aufmachen !".

Ich mußte meinen ganzen Mut zusammennehmen, um diesen Witz in das Buch aufzunehmen. Wie die meisten Witze der Holländer über ihren deutschen oder belgischen Nachbarn, ist er ziemlich derb. Er ist zugleich ein ziemliches Beispiel für schwarzen Humor, aber viele Leute finden ihn lustig. Als ich ihn das erste Mal öffentlich erzählte, war ich in einer Gruppe amerikanischer Betriebswirte, die sich unter der Obhut eines belgischen Professors befanden. Die Amerikaner waren sich nicht sicher, ob sie wegen der Wahrung politischer Korrektheit überhaupt lachen dürften. Der belgische Professor aber, für den Muscheln sowieso eine Gaumenfreude sind, viel vor Lachen fast vom Stuhl. Er rettete mich vor der Blamage.

Wie essen Deutsche Muscheln ?
Sie klopfen auf den Tisch und rufen "Aufmachen !".

Most European countries have their 'Aunt Sallies' - a convenient safety valve for frustration with foreigners. The honour goes to a domestic community, selected more often for slowness of speech than dullness of wit. In France it tends to be the Bretons, in Germany the Ostfrieslanders... and in Switzerland, the Bernese (the Swiss have a good sense of humour too).

There are infinite variations on the Bernese joke. Here are two.

A Bernese trainee paratrooper is told to count to three before pulling the ripcord. Halfway down, he says "one". Just before hitting the ground, parachute unopened, he says "two". On his way to the hospital, he opens his mouth in the ambulance and says "three".

Never tell a Bernese a joke over dinner on Saturday night. He will burst out laughing in church on Sunday.

Ieder Europees land heeft wel een groep die het speciaal moet ontgelden en waar grappen over gemaakt worden. Een handige uitlaatklep voor weerstanden tegen buitenlanders. In Frankrijk treft dit lot de Bretoenen, in Duitsland zijn het de Oost-Friezen en in Zwitserland zijn de mensen uit Bern het mikpunt (ook de Zwitsers hebben gevoel voor humor).

De grappen over de bewoners van Bern zijn onuitputtelijk. Hier zijn twee voorbeelden:

Tijdens zijn opleiding krijgt een marinier uit Bern de opdracht tot drie te tellen voor hij aan het touw van zijn parachute trekt. Als hij halverwege is zegt hij 'één'. Vlak voor hij, nog steeds met een ongeopende parachute, de grond raakt, zegt hij 'twee'. Onderweg naar het ziekenhuis, zegt hij in de ambulance 'drie'.

Vertel iemand uit Bern nooit een grap op zaterdagavond. Want dan barst hij in lachen uit tijdens de preek op zondag.

La plupart des pays européens ont leur têtes de Turc - une excellente soupape de sécurité pour exprimer ses frustrations vis-à-vis des étrangers. En France, cet honneur douteux est dévolu aux Bretons, en Allemagne aux Ostfrieslanders... et en Suisse, aux Bernois (les Suisses ont, eux aussi, un bon sens de l'humour).

Les variations sur le thème de la blague bernoise sont innombrables. En voici deux.

On explique à une recrue paracommando bernoise qu'il doit compter jusqu'à trois avant d'ouvrir son parachute. A mi-parcours, il dit "un". Juste avant de toucher le sol, parachute fermé, il dit "deux". Dans l'ambulance, en route vers l'hôpital, il ouvre la bouche et fait "trois".

Ne racontez jamais une blague à un Bernois au souper du samedi soir. Il risque d'attraper un fou-rire à l'église le dimanche.

Die meisten europäischen Länder haben ihre ganz eigenen "Schießbudenfiguren" — als praktisches Sicherheitsventil für den Ausländern gegenüber empfundenen Frust. Diese Ehre gebührt häufig einer einheimischen Volksgruppe, die eher wegen ihrer bedächtigen Sprechweise als für ihre geistige Unbedarftheit ausgewählt wird. In Frankreich dienen die Bretonen als Zielscheibe, in Deutschland die Ostfriesen... und in der Schweiz schließlich, die Berner (auch die Schweizer haben viel Sinn für Humor).

Die Berner-Witze gibt es in unzähligen Varianten, von denen wir nachstehend zwei erzählen.

Ein Berner Fallschirmjägeraspirant erhält die Anweisung, bis drei zu zählen, ehe er die Reißleine zieht. Auf halbem Weg nach unten sagt er dann 'eins'. Beim Aufschlagen, mit stets geschlossenem Fallschirm, zählt er 'zwei'. In der Ambulanz, auf dem Weg ins Krankenhaus, murmelt er schließlich 'drei'.

Einem Berner darf man nie einen Witz beim Abendessen am Samstag erzählen, weil er sonst am Sonntag in der Kirche vor Lachen brüllt.

When I first starting collecting these jokes, I laboured under the illusion, shared by many Europeans, that the most humourless people in Europe are the German Swiss. Not so. Some of them have a sense of humour which is witty, mordant and (even more surprisingly) understated. Here's an example.

A blind man and his guidedog are standing at a pedestrian crossing. The light turns to green and the dog leads his master across, almost into an accelerating car. On the other side the man gives the dog a biscuit. A passer-by sees this and protests. "But I have to give the dog a biscuit", says the blind man. "Otherwise, how would I know which end to kick?".

❧ ❧

Toen ik begon met het verzamelen van grappen voor dit boek, leed ik aan de misvatting die vele Europeanen met mij delen, dat er in Europa geen volk bestaat met minder gevoel voor humor dan de Duitstalige Zwitsers. Toch is dat niet zo. Er zijn er namelijk bij die van geestige, bijtende en (en wie had dat gedacht) Brits-getinte humor getuigen. Een voorbeeld.

Een blinde man staat met zijn geleidehond bij een zebrapad. Het licht springt op groen en de hond brengt zijn baas naar de overkant, onderweg ze worden daarbij bijna gegrepen door een aanstormende auto. Aan de andere kant van de straat krijgt de hond een koekje van de man. Een voorbijganger die dat ziet, protesteert. "Ik moet die hond wel een koekje geven, antwoordt de blinde. "Want hoe weet ik anders aan welke kant ik hem een trap moet verkopen ?"

Lorsque j'ai commencé à rassembler ces blagues, j'avais l'impression, comme beaucoup d'Européens, que les Européens les plus dénués d'humour sont les Suisses allemands. C'est faux. Certains ont un sens de l'humour spirituel, mordant et (plus surprenant encore) sous-estimé. En voici un exemple.

Un aveugle et son chien-guide se trouvent à un carrefour pour piétons. Le feu passe au vert et le chien mène son maître vers l'autre côté, presque sous les roues d'une voiture. De l'autre côté, l'homme donne au chien un biscuit. Un passant le voit et proteste. "Mais il faut que je donne un biscuit au chien", dit l'aveugle. "Autrement, comment saurais-je de quel côté je dois le frapper ?"

❦ ❦

Als ich damit begann, diese Witze zu sammeln, gab ich mich wie so viele andere Europäer der Illusion hin, das humorloseste Volk in Europa seien die Schwyzerdeutsche. Stimmt nicht, denn manche von ihnen haben einen witzigen, bissigen und (erstaunlicherweise) untertriebenen Sinn für Humor. Hier ist ein Beispiel.

Ein Blinder und sein Hund stehen an einem Zebrastreifen. Die Ampel schaltet auf grün und der Hund führt seinen Herrn über die Straße, fast in die Bahn eines anfahrenden Autos. Auf der anderen Straßenseite angelangt, gibt der Mann dem Hund einen Keks. Ein Passant sieht das und drückt seine Mißbilligung aus. "Aber ich muß doch dem Hund einen Keks geben", sagt der Blinde, "wie soll ich sonst wissen, an welchem Ende ich ihm in den Hintern treten muß ?"

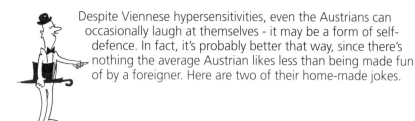

Despite Viennese hypersensitivities, even the Austrians can occasionally laugh at themselves - it may be a form of self-defence. In fact, it's probably better that way, since there's nothing the average Austrian likes less than being made fun of by a foreigner. Here are two of their home-made jokes.

The situation in Germany is serious but not hopeless: the situation in Austria is hopeless but not serious.

We're clever people. We turned Hitler into a German and Beethoven into an Austrian.

Hoewel men er in Wenen niets van moet hebben, zijn er toch Oostenrijkers die soms wel om zichzelf kunnen lachen en misschien is dat wel een vorm van zelfverdediging. En gelukkig maar, want als de gemiddelde Oostenrijker ergens een hekel aan heeft dan is het in zijn hemd gezet te worden door een buitenlander...

De toestand in Duitsland is ernstig, maar niet hopeloos; de toestand in Oostenrijk is hopeloos, maar verder niet ernstig.

We zijn een slim volk: van Hitler maakten we een Duitser en van Beethoven een Oostenrijker.

Malgré les hypersensibilités viennoises, même les Autrichiens peuvent, à l'occasion, se moquer d'eux-mêmes - il pourrait s'agir là d'une forme d'autodéfense. En fait, cela vaut sans doute mieux ainsi, car rien ne déplaît plus à l'Autrichien moyen que d'être raillé par un étranger.

La situation en Allemagne est sérieuse mais pas désespérée; la situation en Autriche est désespérée mais pas sérieuse.

Nous sommes des gens intelligents. Nous avons fait de Hitler un Allemand et de Beethoven un Autrichien.

❧ ❧

Trotz der Überempfindlichkeit der Wiener bringen es sogar die Österreicher fertig, manchmal über sich selbst zu lachen — wohl als eine Art von Notwehr. Wahrscheinlich ist das sehr heilsam, denn was der Durchschnittsösterreicher am wenigsten mag, ist die Schmäh eines Ausländers ...

In Deutschland ist die Lage ernst aber nicht hoffnungslos, in Österreich dagegen ist sie hoffnungslos, aber nicht ernst.

Wir sind ein schlaues Volk. Wir brachten es fertig, Hitler zum Deutschen und Beethoven zum Österreicher zu machen.

The Austrians have a reputation with foreigners for being 'laid back' - and they know it. In July 1976 Vienna's finest bridge over the Danube, the Reichsbrücke, fell into the water. This produced the following joke in the form of a press interview with the mayor of the city:

Journalist: "How could this possibly have happened?"
Mayor: "I've really no idea!"
Journalist: "But don't you have any maintenance procedures?"
Mayor: "Of course we do - for all our bridges!"
Journalist: "But what does this mean?"
Mayor: "We count them once every year!"

✺ ✾

Bij buitenlanders hebben Oostenrijkers de naam 'de zaken niet zo zwaar op te nemen' en daar zijn ze zich terdege van bewust. In Juli 1976 viel in Wenen de mooiste brug over de Donau, de *Reichsbrücke*, in het water.

Dat gaf aanleiding tot de volgende grap in de vorm van een interview met de burgemeester van de stad:

Journalist: "Hoe heeft dit in hemelsnaam kunnen gebeuren?"
Burgemeester: "Ik heb geen idee !"
Journalist: "Maar bestaat er dan geen systeem voor het onderhoud ?"
Burgemeester: "Natuurlijk hebben we dat en voor al onze bruggen."
Journalist: "En waar bestaat dat dan uit ?'
Burgemeester: "Een keer per jaar worden ze geteld !"

Pour les étrangers, les Autrichiens ont la réputation d'être demeurés - et ces derniers le savent. En juillet 1976, le plus beau pont de Vienne au-dessus du Danube, le Reichsbrücke, s'abîma dans les flots. Cet événement produisit l'histoire suivante sous forme d'une entrevue de presse avec le maire de la cité :

Journaliste: "Comment une telle chose a-t-elle pu arriver ?"
Maire: " Je n'en sais absolument rien !"
Journaliste: "Mais vous n'aviez pas de procédures d'entretien ?"
Maire: "Bien sûr que si - et pour tous nos ponts !"
Journaliste: " Et en quoi consistent-elles ?"
Maire: " Nous les comptons une fois par an !"

❧ ❦

Die Österreicher stehen im Ruf, Ausländern gegenüber sehr zurückhaltend zu sein, was ihnen selbst sehr bewußt ist. Im Juli 1976 stürzte die Reichsbrücke, die schönste in ganz Wien, in die Donau. Daraus entstand dann das folgende Interview mit dem Bürgermeister der Stadt :

Journalist: "Wie konnte so etwas bloß passieren ?"
Bürgermeister: "Ich habe wirklich keine Ahnung !"
Journalist: "Haben Sie denn keinen Instandhaltungsdienst ?"
Bürgermeister: "Natürlich haben wir den, für alle unsere Brücken !"
Journalist: "Aus was besteht dieser Dienst ?"
Bürgermeister: "Einmal im Jahr zählen wir alle Brücken !"

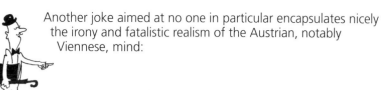

Another joke aimed at no one in particular encapsulates nicely the irony and fatalistic realism of the Austrian, notably Viennese, mind:

Standing on a street corner, Seppl and Rudl observe a group of long-distance runners. "Why are they running like that?", asks Seppl. "They're competing in a marathon", replies Rudl. "But what are they competing for?", persists Seppl. "The one who finishes first gets a prize", replies Rudl, patiently. "OK", says Seppl, "so why are the others competing?"

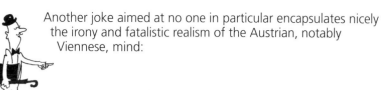

Nog een grap die niemand speciaal op de korrel neemt en toch zeer goed de ironie en de fatalistische realiteitszin van de Oostenrijkers en de Wieners in het bijzonder weergeeft:

Op de hoek van de straat staan Seppl en Rudl te kijken naar een groep lange afstandslopers. "Waarom lopen ze zo hard ?", vraagt Seppl. "Ze doen mee aan een marathon", antwoordt Rudl. "Wat valt er dan te winnen ?", houdt Seppl vol. "Wie het eerste aankomt, krijgt een prijs", antwoordt Rudl geduldig. "Ja, maar", zegt Seppl, "waarom doen die anderen dan mee ?"

Une autre blague sans réel bouc émissaire résume joliment l'ironie et le réalisme fataliste de l'esprit autrichien, notamment viennois :

Seppl and Rudl sont à un coin de rue, d'où ils observent un groupe de coureurs de fond. "Pourquoi courent-ils comme cela ?", demande Seppl. "Ils participent à un marathon", répond Rudl. "Mais pourquoi participent-ils ?", s'obstine Seppl. "Celui qui termine le premier reçoit un prix", répond Rudl, patiemment. "D'accord", dit Seppl, "mais alors, pourquoi les autres participent-ils ?"

❦ ❦

Ein anderer Witz, mit dem eigentlich niemand besonderes gemeint ist, zeigt klar und deutlich die Ironie und den fatalistischen Realismus des Österreichers und ganz besonders des Wieners:

An einer Straßenecke stehen Seppl und Rudl und sehen sich eine Gruppe von Langstreckenläufern an. "Warum rennen die denn so ?", fragt der Seppl. "Die laufen ein Marathon", antwortet der Rudl. "Aber um was geht es denn dabei ?", bohrt der Seppl weiter. "Der Erste bekommt einen Preis", erklärt der Rudl geduldig. "OK", sagt darauf der Seppl, "aber warum laufen denn all die anderen ?".

I first heard this story from a Viennese, but have since heard it from a Hungarian, the only difference between the two versions being that, in the Hungarian version, Otto von H is transmogrified into what I assume is a fictitious character called 'Count Bobby'. Clearly the Hungarians, as much as the Austrians, can claim title to this joke!

Otto von Habsburg, relaxing after dinner, asks his valet to turn on the television set. A football match is in progress. "What's the match?", asks Otto. "Austria-Hungary", replies the valet. "Ah", says Otto, "but who are we playing against?"

❧ ❧

Dit verhaal werd mij voor het eerst verteld door iemand uit Wenen, maar sindsdien heb ik het ook gehoord van een Hongaar. De twee versies verschillen in zoverre dat bij de Hongaren Otto von H een gedaanteverwisseling heeft ondergaan en een soort sprookjesfiguur is geworden die 'Graaf Bobby' heet. Het spreekt vanzelf dat de Hongaren en Oostenrijkers evenveel recht op deze grap kunnen doen gelden.

Otto von Habsburg zit na het diner in de salon en vraagt zijn bediende de televisie aan te zetten. Er wordt een voetbalwedstrijd uitgezonden. "Welke wedstrijd is dat ?" vraagt Otto. "Oostenrijk-Hongarije", antwoordt zijn bediende. 'Oh", zegt Otto, "maar tegen wie spelen wij ?".

C'est un Viennois qui, le premier, m'a raconté cette histoire, mais, par la suite, je l'ai entendue de la bouche d'un Hongrois, la seule différence entre les deux versions étant que, dans la version hongroise, Otto de H. se métamorphose en un personnage, à mon sens fictif, appelé "Comte Bobby". Assurément, les Hongrois, tout autant que les Autrichiens, peuvent revendiquer la propriété de cette blague !

Otto de Habsbourg, qui se relaxe après le dîner, demande à son valet d'allumer la télévision. On donne un match de football. "Quel est ce match ?" demande Otto. "Autriche-Hongrie", répond le valet. "Ah", dit Otto, "mais contre qui jouons-nous ?"

❧ ❦

Diese Geschichte hörte ich zum ersten Mal von einem Wiener, aber dann auch von einem Ungarn und der einzige Unterschied zwischen den beiden Fassungen ist, daß Otto von Habsburg sich in der ungarischen Version auf wunderbare Weise in eine, wie ich annehme, erfundene Persönlichkeit namens "Graf Bobby" verwandelt hat. Sowohl die Ungarn als auch die Österreicher können durchaus Anspruch auf diesen Witz erheben !

Otto von Habsburg gönnt sich etwas Entspannung nach dem Abendessen und bitten seinen Kammerdiener, das Fernsehgerät einzuschalten. Auf dem Schirm sieht man ein Fußballspiel. "Wer spielt ?", fragt Otto, "Österreich-Ungarn" antwortet der Kammerdiener. "Ja schon", sagt Otto daraufhin, "aber gegen wen ?".

Talking about Austria-Hungary reminds me of the story, reputedly true, of the bureaucrat in the old Empire who had two signs on his office door. The first said "Strictly No Admittance!" and the second said "Mind The Step!". This beautifully illustrates the duality of the Central European mind, as does this Hungarian joke told by Georg Kövary.

A group of tourists visit a provincial Hungarian museum. Stopping in front of a showcase containing what is unmistakably a child's skull, the guide proudly announces to the visitors that this is the skull of Kossuth, the great Hungarian hero. When one of the tourists points out that Kossuth died at the age of 92, the guide retorts "this is his skull when he was 12 years old!".

❦ ❦

Het onderwerp Oostenrijk-Hongarije doet me denken aan een ander verhaal, waarvan men beweert dat het waar gebeurd is. Een bureaucraat uit de tijd van de Habsburgmonarchie heeft twee bordjes op zijn deur. Op het eerste bordje staat: "Absoluut geen toegang !" en op het tweede: "Pas op het afstapje !". Dit geeft prachtig het dualisme weer in de Middeneuropese geestesgesteldheid en dat geldt ook voor deze Hongaarse grap van Georg Kövary.

Een groep toeristen brengt een bezoek aan een provinciaal museum ergens in Hongarije. De gids staat stil bij een vitrine waarin een duidelijk herkenbare schedel van een kind ligt. Trots vertelt hij de bezoekers dat dit hier de schedel is van Kossuth, de grote Hongaarse volksheld. Als een van de toeristen te berde brengt dat Kossuth 92 is geworden, krijgt hij ten antwoord "dit is zijn schedel van toen hij 12 was !".

Parler de l'Autriche-Hongrie me rappelle l'histoire prétendument vraie du bureaucrate de l'ancien Empire qui avait deux panneaux sur la porte de son bureau. Le premier disait : "Entrée strictement interdite" et le second "Attention à la marche". Voilà qui illustre magnifiquement la dualité de l'esprit d'Europe centrale, tout comme cette blague hongroise racontée par Georg Kövary.

Un groupe de touristes visite un musée provincial hongrois. S'arrêtant devant une vitrine contenant un objet qui, indéniablement, est un crâne d'enfant, le guide annonce fièrement qu'il s'agit du crâne de Kossuth, le grand héros hongrois. Lorsque l'un des touristes fait remarquer que Kossuth est mort à l'âge de 92 ans, le guide réplique : "eh bien, voici son crâne quand il avait 12 ans !

❦ ❧

Da wir gerade bei Österreich-Ungarn sind, kommt mir die Erinnerung an die als wahr geltende Geschichte des Bürobeamten im vormaligen Kaiserreich, der zwei Schilder an der Tür seines Büros hatte. Auf dem ersten stand "Betreten streng verboten !" und auf dem zweiten "Achtung, Stufe !". Daraus ersieht man wunderbar die Dualität des mitteleuropäischen Geistes, so wie bei diesem, von Georg Kövary erzählten Witz.

Eine Gruppe Touristen besucht ein ungarisches Museum in der Provinz. Die Fremden bleiben vor einer Vitrine stehen, in der sich zweifelsohne der Totenschädel eines Kindes befindet. Der Fremdenführer erklärt den Besuchern mit großem Stolz, dies sei der Totenschädel von Kossuth, dem großen ungarischen Volkshelden. Nachdem einer der Touristen darauf hingewiesen hat, daß Kossuth im Alter von 92 Jahren starb, erwidert der Fremdenführer: "Hier haben wir ja seinen Schädel, als er 12 Jahre alt war !".

There's a 'paired' set of Finnish-Hungarian jokes - maybe I should just say Finno-Ugric - which tell how these two related peoples arrived at the eastern outskirts of Europe and found a stone tablet bearing a message. In the Finnish version of the joke, the message read "Turn right for a nice rich country": the Hungarians couldn't read, so they turned left. In the Hungarian version of the joke, the message read "Turn left for a nice sunny country": in this case it was the Finns who couldn't read.

A Hungarian competing in a Finnish lumberjacking contest astonished his heavyweight hosts by chopping down trees faster than anyone else, despite his modest size. When asked where he learned his trade, he replied: "In the desert". "But there are no trees in the desert!", exclaimed the Finns. "Not now", said the Hungarian.

❧ ❧

Er is een reeks Fins-Hongaarse of eerder Finoegrische tweelinggrappen die vertellen hoe deze twee verwante volkeren in de oostelijke randgebieden van Europa belandden en daar een stenen tafel met inscriptie vonden. In de Finse versie van de grap luidt de boodschap: "Rechtsaf voor een lieflijk en rijk land": en omdat de Hongaren niet konden lezen, gingen ze linksaf. In de Hongaarse versie van de grap luidt de boodschap: "Linksaf voor een lieflijk en zonnig land" en nu waren het de Finnen die niet konden lezen.

Een Hongaar doet mee aan een Finse houthakkerswedstrijd en doet zijn potige gastheren versteld staan, omdat hij het snelste van allemaal bomen kan omhakken, terwijl hij toch klein van stuk is. Als ze hem vragen waar hij het vak geleerd heeft, antwoordt hij: "In de woestijn". "Maar er zijn helemaal geen bomen in de woestijn !", roepen de Finnen. "Nee, nu niet meer", zegt de Hongaar.

Il existe une "combinaison" de deux blagues finno-hongroises - peut-être devrais-je simplement dire finno-ougriennes - qui raconte comment ces deux peuples apparentés arrivèrent aux confins de l'Europe orientale et trouvèrent une tablette de pierre portant un message. Dans la version finnoise de la blague, le message disait : "Tournez à droite et vous trouverez un magnifique pays". Les Hongrois, ne sachant pas lire, tournèrent à gauche. Dans la version hongroise de la blague, le message disait : "Tournez à gauche et vous trouverez un beau pays ensoleillé" : dans ce cas-ci, c'étaient les Finnois qui ne savaient pas lire.

Un Hongrois participant à un concours de bûcherons en Finlande étonna ses poids lourds d'hôtes en abattant les arbres plus vite que quiconque, en dépit de sa constitution modeste. Lorsqu'on lui demanda où il avait appris son métier, il répondit : "Dans le désert". "Mais il n'y a pas d'arbres dans le désert !" s'exclamèrent les Finnois. "Plus maintenant", dit le Hongrois.

Es gibt eine Reihe von finnisch-ungarischen - oder sollte ich sagen finnisch-ugrischen - Witzen, die davon erzählen, wie diese zwei verwandten Völker an den östlichen Rand von Europa gerieten und dort eine Tafel aus Stein mit einer Botschaft fanden. In der finnischen Fassung heißt es in der Botschaft "Nach rechts in die Richtung eines schönen reichen Landes", aber die Ungarn konnten nicht lesen, und bogen deshalb nach links ab. In der ungarischen Version des Witzes befiehlt die Botschaft "Nach links in die Richtung eines schönen sonnigen Landes", aber hier sind es die Finnen, die nicht lesen konnten.

Ein Ungar nimmt an einem finnischen Holzhackerwettkampf teil und fällt zum Erstaunen seiner schwergewichtigen Gastgeber die Bäume schneller als alle anderen, trotz seiner eher bescheidenen Größe. Auf die Frage, wo er das Holzhacken gelernt habe, antwortet er: "In der Wüste". "Aber in der Wüste gibt es doch gar keine Bäume !" , wenden die Finnen ein. "Jetzt wohl nicht mehr", antwortet der Ungar trocken.

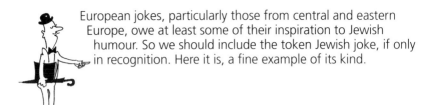

European jokes, particularly those from central and eastern Europe, owe at least some of their inspiration to Jewish humour. So we should include the token Jewish joke, if only in recognition. Here it is, a fine example of its kind.

Q. Why does a Jew always answer a question with a question?

A. And why shouldn't a Jew answer a question with a question?

Europese grappen, vooral als ze afkomstig zijn uit midden- en oost-Europa, zijn zeker voor een deel geïnspireerd op Joodse humor. Dus is een Joodse grap hier niet ontbreken, al was het maar uit erkentelijkheid.

We kozen deze als waardig voorbeeld van het genre.

Vraag: Waarom beantwoordt een Jood een vraag altijd met een vraag ?

Antwoord: Waarom zou een Jood een vraag niet altijd met een vraag beantwoorden ?

En Europe, surtout en Europe centrale et en Europe de l'Est, les blagues doivent ne fût-ce qu'une partie de leur inspiration à l'humour juif. Aussi, nous nous devons de citer une blague juive typique, ne serait-ce que par reconnaissance. La voici, splendide exemple de son espèce.

Q. Pourquoi un Juif répond-il toujours à une question par une autre ?

R. Et pourquoi un Juif ne pourrait-il pas répondre à une question par une autre ?

Europäische Witze, ganz besonders mittel- und osteuropäische, sind zumindest teilweise vom jüdischen Humor inspiriert. Deshalb sollten wir hier symbolisch, mehr als Anerkennung, einen jüdischen Witz einfügen. Hier wäre also dieser Witz, ein hervorragendes Beispiel seiner Art.

Frage: Warum beantwortet ein Jude eine Frage stets mit einer Frage ?

Antwort: Und warum sollte ein Jude eine Frage nicht mit einer Frage beantworten ?

Hungarians have a natural gift for humour, something that has helped them through difficult times (they seem to have been on the wrong side throughout history). The people of Budapest have a particular taste for humour of the black variety. Here's one such joke, also told by Kövary.

A man, thwarted in love, throws himself out of a third-storey window onto the street below. A crowd gathers and a passer-by, curious to know what happened, pushes his way through the crowd and asks what's going on. The dying man opens his eyes and whispers: "I don't know, I just arrived".

❧ ❧

Bij de Hongaren is humor een tweede natuur, wat ze al goed te stade is gekomen in moeilijke tijden (het heeft ze in de loop van de geschiedenis niet meer gezeten). Vooral de inwoners van Budapest hebben een voorkeur voor humor van de zwartste soort. Dit is zo'n grap en komt ook van Kövary.

Een man heeft een ongelukkige liefde en springt van de derde verdieping op straat. Heel wat mensen komen er omheen staan en een voorbijganger, die graag wil weten wat er gebeurd is, duwt de anderen opzij en vraagt wat er gaande is. De man die op sterven na dood is, fluistert: "Ik weet van niets, ik kom net aan".

Les Hongrois sont naturellement doués pour l'humour, ce qui les a aidés à traverser des temps difficiles (ils semblent avoir été du mauvais côté tout au long de l'Histoire). Les gens de Budapest ont une prédilection pour l'humour du type noir. Voici une blague du genre, racontée elle aussi par Kövary.

Un homme, malheureux en amour, se jette du troisième étage. Les badauds l'encerclent et un passant, curieux de savoir ce qui est arrivé, se fraye un passage dans la foule et demande ce qui se passe. Le mourant ouvre les yeux et murmure : "Je ne sais pas, je viens d'arriver".

※ ※

Ungarn haben einen angeborenen Sinn für Humor, was ihnen in schweren Zeiten sehr geholfen hat (besonders weil die Ungarn scheinbar oft auf der falschen Seite standen). Die Einwohner von Budapest lieben ihre eigene Art von schwarzem Humor. Hier ist ein solcher, auch von Kövary erzählter Witz.

Ein unglücklicher Liebhaber springt vom dritten Stock auf die Straße. Eine Menschenmenge strömt zusammen und ein Passant, der wissen möchte, was geschehen ist, drängt sich durch die Leute und fragt, was los sei. Der Sterbende öffnet die Augen und flüstert: "Keine Ahnung, bin selbst gerade erst angekommen".

Most jokes relating to matters behind the old Iron Curtain tended to be self-deprecating, or at least critical of command-economy lifestyles. Queues crop up a lot, as in one example here. Significantly the second joke - which I believe comes from Austria or the USA, and not from Hungary's ex-Comecon neighbours - invokes the image of another 'sequential processing system', the revolving door. The last joke we owe to Flora Lewis' marvellous book, *'Europe: A Tapestry of Nations'*.

What is 100 meters long and eats bread?
A queue outside a Polish butcher's shop.

Who can get into a revolving door behind you and get out in front.
A Hungarian.

The leader of the Soviet Union convoked a Communist summit and put a thumbtack on each delegate's chair to test his responses. The Czech sat down and winced, but held his tongue. The Pole sat down and jumped up with a scream. The Hungarian, never trusting, looked first, discreetly brushed off the tack, sat down and then let out a yell.

❧ ❦

De meeste grappen over de gang van zaken achter het vroegere IJzeren Gordijn getuigden van zelfkritiek of leveren kritiek op de gevolgen van de planeconomie. Er wordt veel in de rij gestaan, de eerste grap is daar een voorbeeld van. Wat opvalt is dat er in de tweede grap sprake is van een ander 'stapsgewijs systeem', de draaideur. De laatste grap is afkomstig uit het prachtige boek van Flora Lewis, *'Europe: A Tapestry of Nations'*.

Wat is 100 meter lang en eet brood ?
De rij voor een Poolse slagerswinkel.

Wie stapt achter u de draaideur binnen en komt er toch voor u weer uit ?
Een Hongaar.

De leider van de Sovjet-Unie riep de Communistische landen voor een top bijeen. Om hun reacties te testen legde hij op de stoel van elke afgevaardigde een punaise. De Tsjech ging zitten, zijn gezicht vertrok van de pijn, maar hij zei niets. De Pool ging zitten en sprong schreeuwend van de pijn weer op. De Hongaar, die van nature wantrouwend is, keek eerst eens, veegde onopvallend de punaise van de stoel, ging zitten en gaf toen een schreeuw van pijn.

La plupart des histoires traitant de ce qui se passait derrière l'ancien rideau de fer tendaient à l'autodépréciation, ou, du moins, à la critique du style de vie en économie planifiée. On y parlait beaucoup de files d'attente, comme dans l'un des exemples ci-dessous. La deuxième histoire est significative d'un autre "système de traitement séquentiel", la porte à tambour. La dernière histoire provient du superbe ouvrage de Flora Lewis, *"Europe: A Tapestry of Nations"*.

Qu'est-ce qui fait 100 mètres de long et mange du pain ?
Une file d'attente devant une boucherie polonaise.

Qui peut rentrer dans une porte à tambour après vous et en ressortir devant vous ? Un Hongrois.

Le dirigeant de l'Union Soviétique avait convoqué un sommet communiste et placé une punaise sur la chaise de chaque délégué pour tester ses réactions. Le Tchèque s'assit et grimaça de douleur, mais ne dit rien. Le Polonais s'assit et sursauta avec un cri. Le Hongrois, toujours méfiant, regarda d'abord, enleva discrètement la punaise, s'assit, puis poussa un hurlement.

᠅ ᠅

Die meisten Witze hinter dem vormaligen eisernen Vorhang neigten dazu, selbstkritisch zu sein, zumindest was das Leben in einem gelenkten Wirtschaftssystem betraf. Schlangestehen wird häufig erwähnt, wie in einem der folgenden Beispiele. Bezeichnenderweise geht es beim zweiten Witz um ein anderes "sequentielles Verarbeitungssystem", nämlich um die Drehtür. Den letzterwähnten Witz verdanken wir dem wunderbaren Buch von Flora Lewis; *"Europe: A Tapestry of Nations"*.

Was ist 100 Meter lang und verzehrt Brot ?
Eine Menschenschlange vor einer polnischen Fleischerei.

Wer kann hinter Ihnen in die Drehtür hinein- und vor Ihnen herausgehen? Ein Ungar.

Der Chef der Sowjetunion beruft eine kommunistische Gipfelversammlung ein und läßt auf jeden Delegiertenstuhl eine Reißzwecke legen, nur um die Reaktionen der Teilnehmer zu beobachten. Der Tscheche setzt sich und verzieht das Gesicht, sagt jedoch keinen Ton. Der Pole schreit und springt auf. Der Ungar, der keinem traut, sieht sich den Stuhl zuerst an, wischt die Reißzwecke weg, setzt sich und stößt dann einen Schrei aus.

 I often wonder what is the logic behind the letters on the test cards and illuminated panels used by opticians to check your eyesight. They seem to change from country to country and from culture to culture. They even seem to change from location to location. Anyway, here's a joke about them.

A Pole goes to have his eyesight checked. The optician hands him a test card and asks him to read it. "Read it?", says the Pole, "I know him!".

 Ik heb me vaak afgevraagd wat de logica is achter de letters op de kaarten en verlichte panelen die opticiens gebruiken bij een ogentest. Er is verschil van land tot land en ook per cultuur zijn er verschillen. Soms lijkt het wel alsof er van plaats tot plaats verschil is. Vandaar dus deze grap.

Een Pool laat zijn ogen testen. De opticien geeft hem een kaart met letters en vraagt hem die op te lezen. "Lezen ?", zegt de Pool, "Die man ken ik!"

Je me demande souvent quelle logique se cache derrière les lettres des cartes-test et des panneaux illuminés utilisés par les opticiens pour contrôler la vue. Il semble qu'ils changent d'un pays et d'une culture à l'autre. On dirait même qu'ils changent d'un endroit à l'autre. Quoi qu'il en soit, voici une blague à leur sujet.

Un Polonais va faire contrôler sa vue. L'opticien lui tend une carte-test et lui demande de la lire. "La lire ?", dit le Polonais, "Je le connais !".

❦ ❧

Mich wundert häufig die Logik der Buchstaben, die auf den Schildern und Leuchttafeln erscheinen, die von Optikern zum Prüfen Ihrer Sehkraft benutzt werden. Sie scheinen von Land zu Land und von Kultur zu Kultur, ja sogar von einer Ortschaft zur anderen verschieden zu sein. Wie dem auch sei, hier ist ein Witz zu diesem Thema.

Ein Pole läßt sein Sehvermögen prüfen. Der Optiker reicht ihm das Testschild und bittet ihn, es abzulesen. "Lesen ?", sagt der Pole, "Kenn ich ihn doch !".

This Albanian proverb says something about the Italians' dislike for bloodletting, mafiosi excepted. It also says something about the talkativeness of the Italians, but even more about the animation and verbosity of the Albanians.

If you want a hundred Italians to be quiet, shoot one.
If you want a hundred Albanians to be quiet, shoot ninety-nine.

Dit Albanese spreekwoord zegt iets over de Italiaanse weerzin tegen bloedvergieten, met uitzondering van de mafiosi dan. Het zegt ook iets over hoe praatgraag de Italianen zijn, maar nog veel meer over hoe levendig en breedsprakig de Albanezen zijn.

Honderd Italianen kun je stil krijgen door er één dood te schieten.

Om honderd Albanezen stil te krijgen, moet je er negen-en-negentig doodschieten.

Ce proverbe albanais donne une petite idée de l'aversion des Italiens, mafiosi exceptés, pour les effusions de sang. Elle donne aussi une petite idée du caractère bavard des Italiens, mais encore plus de l'animation et de la verbosité des Albanais.

Si vous voulez que cent Italiens se taisent, abattez-en un.

Si vous voulez que cent Albanais se taisent, abattez-en 99.

❦ ❦

Dieses albanische Sprichwort läßt die Abneigung der Italiener gegen jedes Blutvergießen erkennen, abgesehen von den Mafiosi. Man ersieht daraus auch die Gesprächigkeit der Italiener, aber mehr noch die Lebhaftigkeit und Langatmigkeit der Albaner.

Will man hundert Italiener zum Schweigen bringen, muß man einen von ihnen erschießen.

Will man hundert Albaner zum Schweigen bringen, muß man neunundneunzig von ihnen erschießen.

117

Even the Greeks can, occasionally, tell jokes at their own expense. This one belies the fabled Greek reputation for hospitality, but it really reflects an antipathy to Albanians (not surprising when there are currently over a million Albanian immigrants looking for work in a country of ten million) and a strange sense of logic akin to that of the Irish.

An Albanian knocks at the door of a Greek farmhouse after a long and tiring journey across the mountains and asks for food. "Sorry", says the Greek, "we've nothing ready. Would would you mind eating yesterday's food?". "Happily!", says the Albanian, his eyes widening in anticipation. "Then come back tomorrow", says the Greek.

❧ ❧

Zelfs de Grieken overkomt het soms wel eens om de draak met zichzelf te steken. Deze grap druist in tegen de befaamde Griekse gastvrijheid, maar geeft blijk van een duidelijke antipathie tegen de Albanezen (wat niet te verwonderen is nu er meer dan een miljoen Albanese immigranten op zoek zijn naar werk in land met 10 miljoen inwoners). En een soort logica waar de Ieren zich zeker in kunnen vinden.

Na een lange en vermoeide tocht door de bergen klopt een Albanees aan bij een Griekse boederij en vraagt om voedsel. "Het spijt me", zegt de Griek, "er is geen eten klaar. Mag het ook eten van gisteren zijn ?" "Graag !", zegt de Albanees reikhalzend. "Kom dan morgen maar terug", zegt de Griek.

Même les Grecs peuvent, à l'occasion, raconter des blagues sur leur propre compte. Celle que voici fait mentir la légendaire réputation d'hospitalité des Grecs, mais reflète en fait une antipathie pour les Albanais (ce qui n'est pas étonnant quand on sait qu'un million d'immigrants albanais cherchent actuellement du travail dans un pays de dix millions d'habitants) et un étrange sens de la logique comparable à celui des Irlandais.

Après un long et fatiguant périple dans les montagnes, un Albanais frappe à la porte d'une ferme grecque et demande à manger. "Désolé", dit le Grec, "nous n'avons rien de prêt. Avez-vous une objection contre la nourriture d'hier ?". "J'en mangerais avec joie !" dit l'Albanais, les yeux agrandis de convoitise. "Alors, revenez demain", dit le Grec.

❧ ❧

Sogar die Griechen bringen es gelegentlich fertig, Witze über sich selbst zu reißen. Dieser Witz verneint den berühmten griechischen Ruf für Gastfreundschaft, aber in Wirklichkeit zeigt er die Abneigung den Albanern gegenüber (kaum verwunderlich wenn man bedenkt, daß gegenwärtig mehr als eine Million eingewanderte Albaner in einem Land mit zehn Millionen Einwohnern auf Arbeitsuche sind) und einen merkwürdigen Sinn für Logik, der an die Iren erinnert.

Ein Albaner klopft nach einer langen und beschwerlichen Wanderung über die Berge an die Tür eines griechischen Bauernhauses und bittet um etwas zu essen. "Tut mir leid", sagt der Grieche, "wir haben nichts fertig. Macht es Dir etwas aus, etwas von gestern zu essen ?". "Aber gerne !", sagt der Albaner, dem beim Gedanken daran die Augen leuchten. "Na, dann komm halt morgen wieder", sagt darauf der Grieche.

To anyone who suggests that humour doesn't cross European frontiers, I say 'look at TV!'. Even the cultural legpulling of 'Allo, Allo' has the French and Dutch laughing as much as the British. And then there is - or was, God rest his soul - Benny Hill. His humour, essentially slapstick, has found its way onto national TV channels in France, the Netherlands, Germany, even Portugal. This is one of his jokes.

A Welshman and a Swede are bragging about their native scenery, trying to top each other's boasts. The Welshman says he can climb to the top of Snowdon, shout "Mister Johnson", and two minutes later the echo repeats "Mister Johnson". The Swede thinks for a moment. "That's nothing," he replies. "In Sweden you climb our mountains, shout 'Mister Yohnson' and three minutes later the echo comes back: 'Which Mister Yohnson you want?'".

Als er beweerd wordt dat humor niet grensoverschrijdend is in Europa, roep ik altijd 'en de tv dan' ! Om de culturele plagerijen in de serie 'Allo, Allo', moeten de Fransen en de Hollanders even hard lachen als de Britten. En dan is er of liever was er, hij ruste in vrede, Benny Hill. Zijn humor, voornamelijk gebaseerd op gooi- en smijtwerk, heeft zich een vaste plaats weten te veroveren op de televisie in Frankrijk, Nederland, Duitsland en Portugal. Dit is één van zijn grappen.

Een man uit Wales en een Zweed zijn aan het opscheppen over het natuurschoon in hun land en proberen elkaar daarbij te overtroeven. De Welshman pocht dat als hij de Snowdon beklimt en "Mister Johnson" roept, twee minuten later de echo terugkomt met "Mister Johnson". De Zweed denkt even na. "Dat stelt niets voor," antwoordt hij. "Als je in Zweden onze bergen beklimt en 'Mister Yohnson' roept, komt er drie minuten later een echo terug die vraagt: "Welke Mister Yohnson moet u hebben ?".

Lorsqu'on prétend que l'humour, en Europe, ne franchit pas les frontières, je réponds : "Voyez la TV !". Même les moqueries d'"Allô, allô" sur les cultures nationales font rire les Français et les Néerlandais tout autant que les Britanniques. Et puis, il y a - ou avait, Dieu ait son âme - Benny Hill. Son humour, essentiellement "tarte à la crème", s'est imposé sur les chaînes télévisées nationales de France, des Pays-Bas, d'Allemagne, et même du Portugal. Voici l'une de ses blagues.

Un Gallois et un Suédois vantent les paysages de leurs pays respectifs, essayant chacun d'avoir le dernier mot. Le Gallois dit qu'il peut monter au sommet du Snowdon, crier "Mister Johnson", et, deux minutes plus tard, l'écho répète "Mister Johnson". Le Suédois reste un moment songeur. "Ce n'est rien du tout", répond-il. "En Suède, vous grimpez nos montagnes, vous criez "Mister Yohnson" et, trois minutes plus tard, l'écho revient : "Quel Mister Yohnson ?".

※ ※

Jedem, der behauptet, daß der Humor in Europa nicht grenzüberschreitend wäre, kann ich nur sagen "Schau Dir die Fernsehprogramme an !". Sogar beim kulturellen "auf den Arm nehmen" wie in der britischen Folge 'Allo, Allo' über die deutsche Besetzung Frankreichs im 2. Weltkrieg bringt die Franzosen und Holländer ebenso zum Lachen wie die Engländer. Und dann gibt oder gab es - Gott sei seiner Seele gnädig - Benny Hill. Sein Slapstick-Humor hat sich auf den nationalen Fernsehkanälen in Frankreich, Holland, Deutschland und sogar Portugal durchsetzen können. Hier ist einer seiner Witze.

Ein Waliser und ein Schwede geben mit der Landschaft ihrer respektiven Heimatländer gewaltig an und jeder bemüht sich, noch besser als der andere aufzuschneiden. Der Waliser erklärt bierernst, er könne auf den Gipfel des Snowdon steigen, laut "Mr. Johnson" rufen und nach zwei Minuten würde das Echo "Mr. Johnson" zurückrufen. Der Schwede denkt etwas nach und sagt dann "Das ist doch gar nichts, in Schweden steigt man auf unsere Berge, schreitet "Mister Yohnson" und nach drei Minuten ruft das Echo zurück: "Welchen Mister Yohnson verlangen Sie ?".

As a change from jokes about national or regional cultures, here's a joke about professional cultures (which, in some organisations, can be even more impermeable than the others). This is the best joke about professional cultures I've heard. It also has the advantage that it's easy to change the order of the professions.

A businessman goes on safari to Borneo and meets a real headhunter who is selling human brains by the kilo. He has lawyers' brains at ECU 10 per kilo, marketing managers' brains at ECU 10 per kilo, and accountants' brains at ECU 20 per kilo. The businessman, surprised that accountants' brains cost twice as much, asks why. "It's simple", says the headhunter, "I have to kill twice as many of them to get a kilo of brains".

❦ ❦

Ter afwisseling van nationale en regionale grappen, nu een grap over beroepsgebonden culturen (die in bepaalde organisaties soms nog ondoorgrondelijker zijn dan de rest). Dit is de beste grap over beroepsculturen die ik ken. En heeft het bijkomende voordeel dat de beroepen verwisselbaar zijn.

Een zakenman gaat op safari naar Borneo en komt daar een heuse koppensneller tegen die menselijke hersenen per kilo te koop aanbiedt. Advocatenhersenen kosten 10 ECU per kilo, 1 kilo marketing managerhersenen kost 10 ECU, accountants-hersenen gaan voor 20 ECU per kilo. De zakenman vraagt verbaasd waarom de accountantshersenen twee keer zo duur zijn. "Dat is nogal logisch", antwoordt de koppensneller, "Voor 1 kilo hersenen moet ik er twee keer zoveel om zeep brengen".

En variante aux blagues sur les cultures nationales ou régionales, voici une blague sur les pratiques professionnelles (qui, dans certaines organisations, peuvent être encore plus imperméables que les autres). C'est la meilleure blague que j'aie entendue à ce sujet.
Elle présente aussi l'avantage qu'il est facile de changer l'ordre des professions.

Un homme d'affaires part en safari à Bornéo et rencontre un véritable chasseur de têtes qui vend des cerveaux humains au kilo. Il a des cerveaux d'avocats à 10 ECU le kilo, des cerveaux de directeurs commerciaux à 10 ECU le kilo, et des cerveaux de comptables à 20 ECU le kilo. L'homme d'affaires, surpris que les cerveaux de comptables soient deux fois plus chers, demande pourquoi. "C'est simple", dit le chasseur de têtes. "Je dois en tuer deux fois plus pour avoir un kilo de cerveaux".

☙ ❧

Als Abwechslung zu Witzen über nationale oder regionale Kulturen, wird hier ein Witz über berufliche Kulturen erzählt (die in manchen Gesellschaften noch undurchlässiger als die anderen sein können). Hier ist der beste, den ich über solche berufliche Kulturen gehört habe. Die Berufe an sich sind natürlich auswechselbar.

Ein Kaufmann nimmt auf Borneo an einer Safari teil und begegnet einem echten Kopfjäger, der menschliches Hirn im Kilo verkauft. Sein Sortiment umfaßt Anwaltshirn zu 10 ECU das Kilo, Hirn vom Marketing Manager zu 10 ECU das Kilo und Hirn vom Buchhalter für 20 ECU das Kilo. Der Kaufmann wundert sich, daß Buchhalterhirn doppelt so teuer ist und fragt nach dem Grund. "Das ist ganz einfach", sagt der Kopfjäger, "Von denen muß ich zweimal so viel fangen, um ein Kilo Hirn zu beschaffen".

This last offering has nothing whatever to do with European cultures, although it includes more than a passing reference to Scotch, as opposed to Scots or Scottish. It is also virtually untranslatable (just as well, since we don't have the space, and it sounds better in English in any case).

"I had twelve bottles of whisky in my cellar, and my wife told me to empty the contents of each and every bottle down the sink, or else... So I said I would, and proceeded with the unpleasant task.

"I withdrew the cork from the first bottle and poured the contents down the sink, with the exception of one glass, which I drank. I extracted the cork from the second bottle and did likewise, with the exception of one glass, which I drank. I then withdrew the cork from the third bottle and emptied the whisky down the sink, with the exception of one glass, which I drank. I pulled the cork from the fourth sink and poured the bottle down the glass, which I drank.

"I pulled the bottle from the cork of the next and drank one sink out of it, and threw the rest down the glass. I pulled the sink out of the next glass and poured the cork down the bottle and drank the glass. I pulled the next cork from my throat and poured the sink down the bottle. Then I corked the sink with the glass, bottled the drink, and drank, the pour.

"When I had everything emptied, I steadied the house with one hand and counted the bottles, corks and glasses and sinks with the other, which were twenty-nine. To be sure, I counted them again, and when they came by I had seventy-four, and as the house came by, I counted again, and finally had all the houses and bottles and corks and glasses and sinks counted, except one house and one bottle which I drank."

Richard Hill

WeEuropeans

Whatever doubts we may have about Maastricht, many of us hold fervently to the idea of a united Europe. And opinion polls among the young show a growing commitment to the European ideal.

This Europe is all about people – people who differ in their tastes and habits but share the same values and ideals. Understanding them, understanding one another, is a crucial step in the process of creating a Europe where unity cohabits with diversity.

Richard Hill talks about the people in this book. He starts by describing, then attacking, the stereotypes and moves on to a witty and skilful analysis of each of the European cultures.

He then enlarges his theme with a comparative analysis of value systems and lifestyles, how people communicate, relate to one another and do business. The final chapter examines recent events and offers thoughts on where we go from here.

"...a fascinating book. His dissection of each nationality produces some wonderful sociological insights."

The European

"Richard Hill starts from the obvious to discover the difficult and makes an impressive success of it."

Emanuele Gazzo, *Agence Europe*

"A delightful and very funny book. I'll buy it!"

Derek Jameson, *BBC Radio 2*

"I can warmly recommend a wonderful book by Richard Hill, 'WeEuropeans'." **Libby Purves,** *BA High Life*

"One of the most interesting books I've ever looked at"
Patrick Middleton, *Riviera Radio*

"Das Buch 'Wir Europäer' des Engländers Richard Hill ist in Brüssel zum absoluten Bestseller avanciert. Mild ironisch analysiert er die Gewohnheiten der Euro-Völker, deckt Gemeinsamkeiten und Unterschiede auf, weist auf Stärken und Schwächen hin"
Birgit Svensson, *Wochenpost*

"Il fallait être Britannique pour oser le pari, il fallait avoir vécu longtemps à Bruxelles pour le réussir. C'est le cas de l'Anglais Richard Hill"
Violaine Muûls, *L'Evénement*

"'WeEuropeans' hoort verplichte lectuur te zijn voor elke deelnemer aan een Eurotop. Het zou de sfeer opvrolijken en de besluitvorming versnellen. De Europeanen, binnen en buiten de EG, zouden er wel bij varen. Om hen gaat het toch altijd, beweren de regeringsleiders onvermoeid"
Henk Aben, *Algemeen Dagblad*

"Wir Europäer: Zum Lachen!"
BZ am Sonntag

"Een onderhoudend boek, dat gezien de huidige ontwikkelingen binnen de Gemeenschap niet alleen actueel, maar ook leerzaam is"
Haye Thomas, *Haagsche Courant*

"I bästsäljaren 'We Europeans' finns vi redan med på ett hörn, som ett hyggligt men gammaldags folk med dörrar som öppnas utåt... 'We Europeans', en munter och innehållsrik bok som snabbt blivit populär bland EG-folket"
Dagens Nyheter, Sweden

"Hill mainitsee sivumennen myös, että suomalaiset juovat paljon. Tämäkin mielikuvaongelma jälleen kerran! Lukiessa eteenpäin käy ilmi, että hän tarkoittaa maidon kulutusta"
Turun Sanomat, Finland

EuroManagers
& Martians
Richard Hill

The Business Cultures of Europe's Trading Nations

EuroManagers & Martians

Looking at them simply as people, when we see them in the streets of Paris or when we visit them *chez eux*, our fellow-Europeans come across as a pretty odd lot – a far cry from the Single Market, harmonisation and all those dreary things.

But how do they behave in business? Put a German, a Frenchman, a Spaniard, an Italian, a Swede and, of course, a Brit together around a negotiating table and what happens? Either nothing at all – they just don't know how to deal with one another – or a lot! It's then that you realise that, despite all the constraints of working within a business environment, life à *l'européenne* is still full of surprises.

The simple fact, of course, is that it would need a super-human to leave his cultural baggage behind him simply because he puts on his coat to go to the office. This book examines the business cultures of Europe's main trading nations and offers useful insights into differences in attitudes to time, hierarchy, protocol, negotiating styles, acceptance of management disciplines and multicultural teamwork.

With so much cultural diversity even in business, the author wonders how on earth we are going to develop the Euromanager we keep hearing about, the person who is going to save us from the Japanese, the Asian Tigers and others. Will this Euro-superman-ager ever exist?

"The book is written from an alien's point of view, and it presents both carefully researched and anecdotal evidence in an entertaining read... Carefully steering a course away from the stereotype path, Hill gives well-considered and practical advice on conducting Eurobusiness." **The European**

'The NewComers'

a book that 'takes the lid off'
the Austrians, Finns and Swedes

Many months after Austria's, Finland's and Sweden's accession to the European Union, ignorance about these countries is as great as ever.

Maybe not where they are, or what they represent economically, but who they are, how they do business, what things are important to them and what are not.

Now Richard Hill and David Haworth, a public affairs consultant specialising in the Nordic countries, have collaborated to write **"The NewComers"**.

This book sets out 'to take the lid off' the Austrians, Finns and Swedes, and explain them to their fellow-Europeans and others. The Norwegians were also supposed to be included but, sadly, things didn't work out that way.

"The NewComers" presents a family portrait of each of the three countries - their virtues, their quirks, tastes, habits and sensitivities, together with background on history and politics.

This book provides even the most mildly curious with a clear and entertaining introduction to those who, from now on, will have a growing influence on the nature of the "new EU".

"I would like to congratulate you on this publication, which is not only a delightful read, but gives at the same time a very comprehensive insight into these countries, their people and mentalities"
Austrian Embassy Official

"Your style is extremely lucid and filled with tolerance and humour. May I inscribe myself in the Richard Hill and David Haworth fan club?" **Swedish lawyer and lobbyist**

"Delightful! You seem to have got the essence of this extremely complex society" **British businesswoman in Vienna**

GREAT BRITAIN
LITTLE ENGLAND

Britons have recently been bombarded and bludgeoned with books examining the reasons for their country's dramatic decline.

But, while offering heavily documented analyses of culprit 'constituencies' - labour, management, educators, civil servants, government itself - these books have stopped short of examining the mindsets, motivations and mannerisms common to the actors in the drama.

In this book, Richard Hill sets out to fill the gap. Starting with himself, he tries to get under the skin of the British - more specifically, the English - and understand where they go right and why they go wrong.

This is an entertaining and thought-provoking book by a Briton who has had the advantage of living outside his island culture, yet consorting closely with it, for the last 30 years.

"I found it fascinating reading. If I weren't British (sorry, English), I would have enjoyed it."

Stanley Crossick,
Belmont European Community Office

"Wonderful stuff. Witty and accurate without being cynical."
John Mole, author of 'Mind Your Manners'

"I am thoroughly enjoying reading it... it cheers up a Scottish Nationalist of a London evening!"

Margaret Ewing, MP

○ **WeEuropeans**
ISBN 90-74440-05-3
BF 700   HFL 38.50 FF 115.-   £13.99   DM 39.90 AS 215.- SFR 29.90

○ **EuroManagers & Martians**
ISBN 90-74440-02-9
BF 695   HFL 38.50 FF 115.-   £12.99   DM 39.90 AS 215.- SFR 29.90

○ **Have You Heard This One?**
An Anthology of European Jokes
ISBN 90-74440-08-8
BF 395   HFL 19.95 FF 65   £ 5.95   DM 18.90 AS 135.- SFR 16.50

○ **Great Britain, Little England**
ISBN 74-4440-04-5
BF 495   HFL 25.-   FF 80.-   £ 9.99   DM 29.90 AS 165.- SFR 24.90

○ **The NewComers**
ISBN 90-74440-06-1
BF 595   HFL 29.90 FF 90.-   £ 10.99 DM 34.-   AS 195.- SFR 28.50

Other books on European cultures are in preparation.

If you have difficulty in obtaining any of these books through your local bookstore, you can order through the publisher:

Europublic SA / NV,
Avenue Winston Churchill 11 (box 21), B-1180 Brussels
Tel. +32-2-343.77.26 - Fax +32-2-343.93.30

Name: ....

Address:...

....

....

Tel:................................. Fax: ....

'WeEuropeans', 'EuroManagers & Martians' and other Europublic books have been selected as course material by the following institutions:

BELGIUM	Antwerp University (UFSIA), English Dept. Erasmus Hogeschool, Brussels Gent University, Department of Sociology Hoge Technische Instituut, Brugge ICHEC Business School, Brussels Institut für Erwachsenenbildung, Eupen/St Vith ISC Saint-Louis Business School, Brussels KUL Leuven KVH Interpreters School, Antwerp Solvay Business School (ULB), MEB Programme United Business Institutes, Brussels Université de Mons, Sciences Economiques
BRITAIN	Institute of Management (IM) The Centre for International Briefing The Open University
DENMARK	Copenhagen Business High School
FINLAND	Helsinki Institute Jyväskylä University, European Studies Vaasa University, European Studies
FRANCE	Groupe ESC, Lyon INSEAD, Fontainebleau Université de Nancy II
GERMANY	Hochschule der Künste, Berlin Mercator Universität, Duisburg
NETHERLANDS	HEAO business course Netherlands Institute for MBA Studies, Utrecht
SWEDEN	Swedish Institute of Management (IFL) University of Lund
USA	Antioch University, Ohio Chicago University, Graduate School of Business Massachusetts University (Plymouth) Michigan State University New York University, Stern School of Business Temple University School of Business and Management, Philadelphia UCI Graduate School of Management, Irvine (CA) University of Pennsylvania Wright State University, Ohio **… and the training arms of various international corporations.**

Services Available

Europublic represents the author of this book, Richard Hill, as well as other specialists in European affairs.

In addition to book publishing, Europublic provides speakers on cross-cultural topics and conducts tailored in-company training courses on cultural issues impacting on organisations operating in an international and multicultural environment.

In addition to lecturing at various European and US universities and business schools, Europublic specialists act as speakers and consultants with various organisations in both the public and private sectors. These include the European Commission, the Helsinki Institute, the 'Eurochannels' conference organisation, Citibank, GE Capital, the IBM International Education Centre, Medtronic, Pioneer, Price Waterhouse and 3Com Europe.

For further information on these services, please mail or fax to:

Europublic SA/NV
Avenue W. Churchill 11 (box 21)
B - 1180 Brussels
Tel: +32-2-343.77.26
Fax: +32-2-343.93.30

VISIT US IN CYBERSPACE:

Europublications is interested in hearing of other European jokes. The only proviso is that they should be (1) funny, (2) not too abusive and (3) translatable. If you know of any, please tell us about them with the help of this form.
We will be happy to print them, acknowledged, in a future edition. Thanks!

Europublic SA/NV, Avenue Winston Churchill 11 (box 21), B-1180 Brussels. Fax: + 32-2-343.93.30

You may like to consider the following European joke for inclusion in your next edition (please state origin if known):

....

....

....

....

....

Name: ....

Address: ....

....

....